TRADITIONALISM: THE ONLY RADICALISM

JOHN DUNN

First published in 2014 by the Study Press, London.

Ninth printing (2020).

Typeset in Palatino by the Study Press. Printed and bound by Book Printing UK, Peterborough, England.

© John Dunn

A CIP record for this book is available from the British Library.

ISBN 978-0-9928877-0-4

Dedicated to the memory of my mother.

Contents

Contents

Preface

It is a feature of twenty first century modernity that the tenets around which society is built and organised exist unchallenged.

When there is only one cultural perspective and no alternative story, where is the judgement about the worth of the existing regime meant to come from?

The left-right political dichotomy serves liberalism by not challenging it. Democracy sustains the status quo by offering the illusion of choice with no choice.

Genuine opposition can only emerge if there is an alternative story with which to counter the current mythos.

And how that mythos is maintained! By the great world enterprise, with its digital mountain of media propaganda, Hollywood-fashioned histories, global corporate HR masquerading as an education system and pseudo-religious convictions riddled with liberal 'ethics'. Against this multi-billion dollar programme of maintenance, a few mere words could hardly be said to endanger the global regime.

Yet I contend that the weakness of liberalism lies in the shallowness of its roots. The belief in its apparent virtues can only be sustained by lies, and even these cannot disguise liberalism's materialistic origins and sustaining raison d'être. Those who live under its all-seeing eye are left either consciously bereft of meaning or deluded into laughing despair.

The world state cannot be opposed from outside. There is no longer any outside. Yet the opposition that must come from within is fragmented. Redemption will not be possible until today's heresies coalesce into a new mythos.

Enough of scholarship therefore, what we need is original work to expose the essential wheel in the working of things, the eternal struggle between good and evil. Only then will moral choice be clear and a meaningful political dichotomy emerge, with sufficient distance to make liberalism the other.

This book was inspired by the hope of contributing towards the redemptive coalescence of thought and deed.

1 Introduction

We swim in the medium of liberalism. Throughout our school and working lives, the non-discriminative principles, known euphemistically as 'political correctness', are drilled into us. In a Hollywood-Disneyland world of media stereotypes, the 'good' guys always win, where the good is equated with the liberal and 'progressive'; and the cops get the villains, leaving the world a safer place for homo economicus to pursue his nihilistic dreams.

Little wonder that our western way of life appears rational, even natural, and the culmination of a long chain of Darwinistic evolutionary progress. The hard fact to swallow is that it is none of these. Liberalism, the dominant western, verging on global, belief system is built on a chimera, a lie.

Liberalism's mantra of equality has arisen in such a manner that no other difference is acknowledged to be more right and more true than that which is 'achieved' through one's efforts and 'merit', according to the terms of liberalism's monetary measure of value.

From a higher point of view (from a point of view that knows that the progressive decay of the organism will eventually push one into nothingness), meritocracy and the chasing after wealth, or self-fulfilment, or peer-recognition, or celebrity, all lead, quite literally, to dead ends.

Yet liberalism remains unchallenged from any point of view. The political left and right in the West are both sides of the same coin. Where one promotes multi-culturalism, the other offers globalisation. The same applies to nationalisation and corporatisation, equality and commoditisation, liberty and the free market, materialism and the amoral economic space, education and media indoctrination. Even Karl Marx was pro-capitalism to the extent that it was necessary to sweep away tradition. Where religion exists in the West, it is these days founded upon ambiguously liberal 'ethics'. It is not a coincidence either that vaguely left causes are often supported by the global elite.

In short, the same coin is liberalism and there is no opposition to it. The political right in the West was long ago hijacked by economic liberalism. And what does liberalism serve? Money. It arose out of financial liberalism, the freedom to make money out of money. Whatever the personal belief held by the individual, whatever the motive driving the individual, the way society is constituted under liberalism means that his or her efforts will serve money in the end.

'Thank God for the possibility of my holding certain beliefs' some might say. But it is too simplistic to suggest that all are at liberty to think how they will. You only have to look at the world to see that people are thinking, behaving and consuming in ways that are increasingly similar. Liberty seems to be mistaken for the 'principles' of the corporate human resources department, where all are equal in a 1=1 prison. In this sense, an individual right becomes a right to nothing.

We might be free to hold beliefs, even if under strict surveillance, but these will eventually be an irrelevance. It is much easier and safer to be like all the others, to become a repetition, a number along with the crowd, all serving the great global enterprise in the most efficient manner. Belief will become a folk memory.

Being two sides of the same coin, today's political left and right offer a false dichotomy. The right has been hijacked by economic liberalism, whereas once it was resistance to the amoral economic space opened up by money that motivated the radical right.

A renewed political dichotomy would have the liberal economic motive on one side and the ethically-driven on the other, the latter founded on beliefs that have a transcendental origin, separate to man. Without a renewed political dichotomy, there will be no opposition to liberalism in the West. But how will one emerge? All contact with previous eras of faith have been lost; the distance between the traditional and today's egoistic mind being vast.

The answer is that faith and tradition will have to be rediscovered and relearnt. This will have to happen outside of academia, which is now merely a functionary of liberalism, engaged in the business of preparing workers for the wage economy.

Once a process of rediscovery has been undertaken, then a more meaningful and historically relevant political dichotomy will arise in the form of liberalism versus traditionalism, the latter being the radical challenger to the status quo. Traditionalism is the only radicalism.

2 Papering over the cracks of Kierkegaardian despair

Modern liberal democracy appears to be the natural outcome of a long and inevitable process of history, the final flowering of rationality out of the dark millennia of superstition. Indeed, even to question this seem alien, even dangerous to our rational western minds. Is not our western rationality precious after all? The very fruits of it, for example science, democracy and education, the component parts of liberalism, are surely the future of a world in which freedom and human rights are to be enjoyed by all, and for which people are sacrificing their lives today? It is upon enlightened rationality, the end-product of inevitable progress, that liberalism stands now and for millennia ahead, if Hollywood is to be believed. Traditionalism challenges this acquiescence to 'progress'.

Liberalism has its roots in Plato, Aristotle, Augustine and, later, Descartes, amongst others; a mode of thought that is founded on a dualism of mind and body, or mind and material world. It is inculcated into us, from birth and through all the separated disciplines of the education system, that we are all disembodied subjects (Augustine would extend this principle into the form of an eternal soul), observing and negotiating objects, the material

5

world external to the mind. This historical separation of mind and body or world, this opposition of an interior life to an external world, would lead ultimately to our sense of individuality, the individualism of modern times.

The dualism of mind and material world became manifest in the the separation of the economic sphere from the religious and moral sphere, leaving the individual at least notionally free to lead a parallel desacralised life, accumulating wealth in a way that would have been once abhorrent to the church and society at large in the pre-Reformation world. For a life led in pursuit of financial gain was considered sinful, and gain through usury, the lending of money for interest, the worst form of this avaricious sin. A dualistic life was not considered sustainable by Christ's own precepts. 'No man can serve two masters: for either he will hate the one, and love the other; or else he will hold to the one, and despise the other. Ye cannot serve God and mammon.' *Matthew* 24.

The dualism was manifested too in political struggle, with an individual liberty, based on the claim that introspectively based judgements about one's own mental states are infallible, underpinning the related philosophies of liberalism, Marxism and anarchism.

And, of course, it is Cartesianism dualism that underpins science; it is the very foundation of today's scientific worldview, one in which the disembodied observing subject seeks to understand all it can about the objective state of the material world external to it, through experiment and measurement. Measured in quantity against a human scale, science has met with a success that has served to reinforce Cartesian dualism as the unquestioned mode of modern thought. And why not? Has not western rationality since the renaissance given us democracy and freedom of thought and expression? Then there are the benefits of modern medicine; and has not scientific progress fed and clothed us and kept us warm? Would we not put all this at risk by questioning the very mode of thinking that achieved it all? Surely we should all spring to the defence of our western way of life whenever it is under threat, and aid those who want to throw off whatever tyrannical yoke they are under in order to join us in our liberty.

And yet, what is this disembodied mind of western rationality? Nothing, argues the Cartesian position itself, most famously championed by John Locke. It is a 'tabula rasa', to be filled in by whatever worldly experience happens to come its way, for from where else might ideas and influences come if not this world? That the individual is a passive receptor is the implication of this position, a state of affairs which is distinctly at odds with the western mind's avowed defense of individual freedom.

Oh the quest for knowledge, with which our minds are imbued, it fills not the emptiness, it simply hides it and buries the despair. If we commence life as a void, upon what is our knowledge grounded? More knowledge simply raises to consciousness our own innate emptiness. From the Cartesian standpoint, we are born into a fixed and finished world, there to labour within the strict confines of a mind-independent reality. Could there be a more cruel, elaborate and stultifying fiction? To be thrust at birth into a prefabricated external world, where most of our responsibilities are unacknowledged and are progressively diminished and our freedom is in reality a figment of our imagination. We imagine ourselves the product of genes and the environment, functions of complexes and familial trauma, inextricably dependent on external contingencies, but then proclaim ourselves free!

To hold a conviction that we can only come to know the world by observing it as spectators is to prescind from a direct, active and moral involvement. It is the very opposite of freedom. Perhaps we should not be surprised after all that western rationality, with its credo of liberalism and individual freedom, has led to inhumanness and sameness the world over. The paradox is that this sameness is all-pervasive under liberalism, a political creed that proclaims individual liberty. And it is about more than mere imposition of global uniformity, it is about the loss of self. Under the individualism of modern times, the authentic self has disappeared.

This paradox takes us right to the heart of Søren Kierkegaard's radical critique of social conformity. If those of an atheistic temperament are to fully appreciate his contribution to thought as the founder of existentialism, they must substitute God with the truth, that in which the innate convictions of conscience held by the self are grounded. Kierkegaard defined the self as a conscious synthesis of the infinite/finite, the temporal/ eternal and freedom/necessity, all in relationship to God, who is the Source and End of self-conscious life. We will be in a state of 'despair' when we attempt to deny any one of these paradoxes and thereby choose to understand ourselves apart from a relationship with God.

And what is living apart from God? What are the implications for the individual who denies the innate convictions of conscience? Kierkegaard explains:

> ... by being busied with all sorts of worldly affairs, by being wise to the ways of the world, such a person forgets himself, in a divine sense forgets his own name, dares not believe in himself, finds being himself too risky, finds it much easier and safer to be like all the others, to become a copy, a number, along with the crowd.

> Now this form of despair goes practically unnoticed in the world. Precisely by losing himself in this way, such a person gains all that is required for a flawless performance in everyday life, yes, for making a great success out of life... He is ground as smooth as a pebble, as exchangeable as a coin of the realm. Far from anyone thinking him to be in despair, he is just what a human being ought to be... A man in this kind of despair can very well live on in

*temporality; indeed he can do so all the more easily,
be to all appearances a human being, praised by
others, honoured and esteemed, occupied with all
the goals of temporal life. Yes, what we call
worldliness simply consists of such people who, if
one may so express it, pawn themselves to the
world. They use their abilities, amass wealth, carry
out enterprises, make prudent calculations etc., and
perhaps are mentioned in history, but they are not
themselves. In a spiritual sense they have no self, no
self for whose sake they could venture everything,
no self for God - however selfish they are otherwise.*[1]

Wait a minute, did not Karl Marx consider religion itself
to be an inauthentic way of coming to terms with a heartless world? Wasn't it the ultimate way of dulling the self
against the anxieties of the world, the ultimate analgesic,
the 'opium of the people'?

Surely, implied Marx, the authentic person is the one free
of God. But what then is such an opium-free self, the
'clean' self, the authentic self? Well surely it begins on
day one of the truly post-revolutionary world under
communism, the moment perhaps when the state will
have 'withered away'. What will the authentic individual
do at that moment? Well, according to Marx, he will do
what he likes.

---

[1] S. Kierkegaard, *Provocations: Spiritual Writings of Kierkegaard*, C. E.
Moore ed., Plough Publishing, New York, 2002 pp.136-7

Perhaps Marx's best known statement on this subject is his claim that

> ...*in communist society, where nobody has one exclusive sphere of activity but each can become accomplished in any branch he wished, society regulates the general production and thus makes it possible for me to do one thing today and another tomorrow, to hunt in the morning, fish in the afternoon, rear cattle in the evening, criticize after dinner, just as I have a mind, without ever becoming hunter, fisherman, shepherd, or critic.*[2]

Yet what are these accomplishments if not various ways of papering over the cracks of Kierkegaardian despair. Given the direction of modern liberal society, I would contend that people in such conditions will end up doing the same things as everyone else. But even if not, their accomplishments will be so many ways of forgetting the self and distractions from the inevitability of death in the busying of the self. With regard to the authentic life, communism would change nothing. Marx himself said that under capitalism, 'all that is holy' would eventually be 'profaned', and how right he was. But the profanation of religion would not lead men and women to face the truth in Kierkegaardian terms, far from it. Communism, as Marx envisaged it, would simply give people more

---

[2] Karl Marx and Friedrich Engels, *German Ideology, Part 1 and Selections from Parts 2 and 3*, ed. Christopher John Arthur, International Publishers, New York, 2004, p. 53.

opportunities to be distracted from the truth in worldly accomplishments devoid of God.

3 An eternal inauthenticity

Marx, in his vision of a communist life as the accumulation of accomplishments, took liberalism to its utmost extent, positing that the authentic self is to be found in conditions which facilitate a complete freedom of choice. These conditions are communism, perhaps better understood in its original Marxian intent if described as anarchism. Only in conditions of complete freedom for the individual, to this way of thinking, can the alienated subject be recovered and the historical process of individuation be completed, allowing the individual to emerge finally from the herd as a fully-rounded and fulfilled human being.

The paradox of liberal society, where individuality has led to a tendency of sameness the world over, suggests that the opposite will happen and the individual will sink back into the herd.

The pursuit of fulfilment supposedly made possible under communism, cannot overcome the Kierkegaardian objection that the piling up of accomplishments would be merely a distraction from despair and an indication that the self has been lost. It could never offer a life that is honest in the face of death or God. The pursuit of a fulfilled life would become a new fetish, a false god to be worshipped by the apparently free individual. It would be a thing apart from the individual, offering a goal to be attained, yet trapping the individual in an ideology of success no less invidious than that which already exists under market capitalism. A dualistic distraction would emerge, a chasm separating the subjective self from the prospect of a fulfilled self.

So blinkered down a path of worldly achievement is modern man that it is not until the very point of death that all the distractions, ambitions, aspirations and flight to the crowd cease to have their analgesic effect and he wakes to the truth of being. Martin Heidegger wrote of this very moment in his *History and the Concept of Time*, the dread of death - the point of death when the individual is exposed as what he really is. Heidegger wrote, 'there is thus the possibility, in the very moment of departing from the world, so to speak, when the world has nothing more to say to us and every other has nothing more to say, that the world and our being-in-it show themselves purely and simply.'[3] The flight of the individual from himself has to end. At the point of death he has no choice but to confront himself. The individual sees himself in all his nakedness. In this we are reminded of the words from Job 1:21, 'Naked came I out of my mother's womb, and naked shall I return thither: the Lord gave, and the Lord

---

[3] M. Heidegger, *History of the Concept of Time: Prolegomena*, Indiana University Press, 1992, p.291

hath taken away; blessed be the name of the Lord.' At the point of death, flight is no longer an option. The difference between modern and traditional man is that the latter never thought it was in the first place.

'Das Man', Heidegger's expression for the multitude of people around the individual, tries to steal authenticity away by covering up death with platitudes such as, 'well everyone dies'. 'Everyone dies', in this context, is about offering the delusion that no one dies. In giving in to that way of thinking, the crowd covers up the authenticity of death.

The idea of not being in the world, Heidegger argued, is something that the individual has to wrestle with before arriving at the realisation that death is always an imminent possibility, the ever-present fact that never goes away. Out of the struggle with this realisation can come the drive for the creation of an authentic life that will truly differentiate the individual from the crowd, the one from the everyone.

Death has been the underlying motivating factor of all the higher cultures throughout history and pre-history. Most of the archaeological remains of the earliest cultures are associated with death. Be it the Egyptians with their cult of mummification, or the Hindus with their ceremonial burning of the dead, each civilisation centres on an agreed ceremonial mode of the disposal of the dead. Looking back to the Paleolithic era, it is the burial site that is associated with the very beginnings of human culture. One is tempted to say, in the light of Heidegger's work, that the life led by Stone Age man was a much more authentic one than the life led by contemporary 'Das Man'.

Despite the utter futility of striving to be materially different in a world that ruthlessly imposes uniformity, conformity and commoditisation, a self-misperception of individuality often survives to the very end of life. I am reminded of a most hideous manifestation of this in crematoria up and down the land, where families and friends celebrate the 'defiant' departed's success (in Kierkegaardian terms, conformity), by playing a trashy pop song favourite of the loved one as the curtain closes on the coffin. This is the pitiful pseudo-defiance of a Don Giovani, foisted upon the dead by the ignorant and fearful survivors. It is the continued flight to 'Das Man' of those who remain, or even the pursuit by 'Das Man' of the dead beyond the grave to an eternal inauthenticity, analogous with Hell.

Any celebration of the dead departed's meritocratic achievement in reality masks a terror of annihilation amongst those left behind, a reinforcement of 'all that is required for that flawless performance in everyday life, for making a great success out of life', as Kierkegaard described it, 'to become a repetition, a number along with the crowd' to be 'ground as smooth as a pebble'. In the clamour to praise what a person ought to be, the self is literally crowded out of the collective consciousness and the very being in human is lost as a result. Authenticity is lost; truth is lost.

Such is the depth of the Kali Yuga into which the modern world has sunk. We arrived at this flight from authenticity, the masking of truth, by a route other than that delineated by liberalism's official histories. There has been a process of regression rather than progress, decline rather than advancement. A recovery of the authentic history is therefore vital to the positing of a new and meaningful political dichotomy, in which traditionalism can confront a liberalism that is exposed as being flawed from the start.

4 Life as rite, not flight

In contrast to modernity, the lives of tradition were led as rite, not flight, and social institutions assumed a sacramental character, for they were the outward and imperfect expressions of a supreme spiritual reality.

The medieval society of Christendom was structured as a single social organism, expressing the need for co-operation among the individual organs and parts in the unity of the whole. It was a living acknowledgement of St. Paul's admonishment 'that there may be no division in the body, but that the parts may have the same concern for one another' (1 Corinthians 12:25). 'Indeed, the parts of the body that seem to be weaker are all the more necessary' (1 Corinthians 12:22). We are, St Paul adds, 'individually parts of one another' (Romans 12:5) in the body of Christ, the Church. The multiplicity of the members and the variety of their functions could never damage this unity, just as, on the other hand, this unity could not cancel or destroy the multiplicity and variety of the members and their functions.

The need for biological harmony in the human organism was applied analogously in theological language to indicate the necessity of solidarity among all the members of the Church community. 'If one part suffers', said St. Paul, 'all the parts suffer with it; if one part is honoured, all the parts share its joy' (1 Cor 12:26).

Each member of the social organism had its own function: prayer, or defence, or merchandise, or tilling soil. Each received the means suited to its station, and claimed no more. Within classes there was equality; if one took into his hand the living of two, his neighbours would go short. Between classes there had to be inequality; for otherwise a class could not perform its function, or - a strange thought to us - enjoy its rights. Peasants were not to encroach on those above them. Lords had not to despoil peasants. Craftsmen and merchants had to receive what would maintain them in their calling, and no more.

Regardless of its place in the hierarchy of functions, each activity was of value on its own plane, provided that it was governed, however remotely, by the end which was common to all; and that end was an authentic life, salvation. Like the celestial order of which it was but a dim reflection, society was stable because there was a common cause in the straining upwards.

The structuring of society as a single social organism had universalist principles. Taking the caste system of Hindu India as his prime example of a traditional society, Julius Evola explained how 'every type of function and activity appeared equally as a point of departure for an elevation in a different and vertical rather than horizontal sense'.

Emphasising the unity of the social organism, he described how 'everybody performed their function within the overall social order, and through their own peculiar bhakti even partook of the supernatural principle of this same order'.[4]

There was no place either in Christian medieval life for any economic activity which was not related to a sacred end. It is important to understand the holistic nature of this worldview, for it was the totality of traditional society that distinguished it from the modern world, which would eventually fragment tradition's authority. The material was ordained for the sake of the spiritual; economic goods were instrumental. 'It is lawful to desire temporal blessings', said St Thomas Aquinas, 'not putting them in the first place, as though setting up our rest in them, but regarding them as aids to blessedness, inasmuch as they support our corporal life and serve as instruments for acts of virtue.'[5] 'Riches, as St Antonino commented, exist for man, not man for riches.'[6]

All activities fell within an all-embracing system, because the members of society, regardless of hierarchy, were united by the goal of salvation and derived their authenticity from

---

[4] J. Evola, *Revolt Against the Modern World*, Inner Traditions International, Vermont, 1995, p.95

[5] Quoted in R.H. Tawney, *Religion and the Rise of Capitalism*, Pelican, Harmondsworth, 1961, p.44

[6] Tawney p.44

it. The Church as the body of Christ offered the doctrine through which that goal was realised. As head of the Church, Christ was the principle and source of cohesion among the members of his body (cf. Col 2:19). He was the principle and source of growth in the Spirit: from him the entire body grew and built 'itself up in love' (Eph 4:16). This was the reason for the Apostle's exhortation to live the truth in love' (Eph 4:15). The spiritual growth of the Church's body and its individual members was a growth 'from Christ' (the principle) and also 'into Christ' (the goal). The Church embraced the whole of life and its authority was final. This meant, as R. H. Tawney put it, that there was 'no absolute division between the inner and personal life, which is the "sphere of religion", and the practical interests, the external order, the impersonal mechanism, to which, if some modern teachers may be trusted, religion is irrelevant.'[7]

The unity of religious and material life had universalist principles which are found 'in the notion of dharma, or one's peculiar nature to which one is supposed to be faithful'.[8] Evola explained that the dharma of the Hindus came 'from the root dr ("to sustain", "to uphold") and it expresses the element of order, form, or cosmos that Tradition embodies and implements over and against chaos and becoming. Through *dharma* the traditional world, just

---

[7] Tawney p.33

[8] Evola p.95

like every living thing and every being, is upheld; the dams holding back the sea of pure contingency and temporality stand firm; living beings partake of stability'.[9]

Given the importance of dharma to social cohesiveness and hence to spiritual elevation, it is clear why not being faithful to oneself, by departing from the functions and obligations of caste, 'was considered a sacrilege that destroys the efficacy of every rite and leads those who are guilty of it to "hell".... The people guilty of crossing the "caste line" were considered the only impure beings in the entire hierarchy; they were pariahs, or "untouchables" because they represented centres of psychic infection in the sense of an inner dissolution'.[10] Such was the opprobrium in which practical interests to the exclusion of religion were held, that the people who practised these activities were held to be social outcasts. They were isolated out of the fear that infection, in the form of purely contingent and temporal activity, entering one part of the social organism threatened deathly disease to the rest.

Any economic activity which was not related to a moral end was considered as a degrading form of escapism. It forced a wedge between the inner life and the external order, splitting the totalising social system through which men derived their authenticity and putting at threat the ultimate

---

[9] Evola p.95

[10] Evola p.96

goal of salvation. 'The outcast was just the vanquished - in the Aryan East he was called a fallen one, patitas.'[11]

Members of the social organism attempted to spiritualise the material by incorporating it in a divine universe, which should absorb and transform it. To that process of trans-mutation, the life of mere money-making was recalcitrant, hence the stigma attached to it. This found practical expression in Medieval Europe in the forbidding of the business of usury to Christians. For usury was considered to be a sin, on a par with adultery and fornication in its threat to social cohesiveness.

In the Christian mind, there was an opposition between the world, understood as the human sphere, the totality of man on the one hand, and the sphere of God on the other. The former was conceived as under the domination of 'the prince of the world' or 'the god of this world', who was the enemy of God (John 12.31; II Cor. 4.4). The world threatened to dominate and rule over the individuals who constituted it. 'The spirit of the world' lay over men (I Cor. 2.12). The relation of the Christian to the world was that whilst he had overcome the world and been freed from its tyranny, he remained in the world so long as he existed on earth, continually exposed to its threat (I Cor. 3.21-22: John 17.11). The usurers would typically be non-participants in the body of the Church, namely Jews. As outcasts and threats to society and the salvation of its

[11] Evola p.96

members, they would be feared as associates of the prince of the world.[12]

---

[12] See J. Trachtenberg, *The Devil and the Jews*, The Jewish Publication Society, Philadelphia, 1995

5 Defence against the encroachment of barbarism

The very idea of engagement in economic activity for its own ends, completely divorced from moral ends, simply did not exist in the minds of the general medieval populace. The idea that individuals might have an inborn appetite for personal economic gain, and might therefore be thought of as rational players in a system of economics founded upon individual economic choices, would have been thought of as irrational, let alone immoral, if it could have been countenanced at all. To found a social philosophy upon individual economic motives would have been considered as base and brutish as as we might think a system of human organisation based upon sexual instincts, only more so.

The non-productive ways in which an individual might seek to acquire or increase his holding of wealth, whether by buying and selling or lending and borrowing, were lumped together by the Church as avarice, or greed, one of the seven deadly sins. This was especially so amongst the merchants, grocers and victualers who conspired to create local monopolies and cartels, or money-lenders who ground down the poor. For this reason, in what was essentially a pre-money society, with currency a small, but stable adjunct to to an agrarian economy, any price rises would be looked upon with huge suspicion. Chaucer's *The Pardoner's Tale* contains a sermon against avarice, and traders caught using false scales or adulterating food were excommunicated, pilloried, put in the stocks or banished from towns.

Indeed, when wrong-doing was suspected, then it was a sacramental action to stand the culprit in the pillory. A taverner might be forced to drink huge quantities of his own adulterated wine. A baker selling adulterated or short-weight bread, might have a token loaf hung around his neck, and then be dragged down the street. Whilst all this was going on, the parish priest might deliver a sermon on the sixth commandment, choosing as his text the words of the Book of Proverbs, 'Give me neither riches nor poverty, but enough for my sustenance'.[13]

There was an abhorrence of avarice because the social ethics consisted in realising one's being and achieving one's perfection within the parameters of that part of the social organism to which one belonged. Economic activity was justified only to the extent that it was necessary for sustenance and to ensure the dignity of an existence which conformed to one's own estate, without the base instinct of self-interest or material gain coming first.

---

[13] Tawney p.67

In the Middle Ages, the ascetic temper predominated in Christian sentiments, which contributed to the concept of society as a spiritual organism, not an economic machine. Material appetites and the desire for economic gain were rooted in the doctrine of original sin and were, as a consequence, sinful. Necessary economic activity, like the sexual instinct, was one subordinate part of a complex whole and, like all other activities in the ascetic life of man lived as rite, had to be kept to its moral ends through a strict repression of its worldly tendency to grow and become all-consuming of lives and minds. To think otherwise would have been to give in to barbarism.

Honorius Augustodunensis for example, saw nothing in economic life but the struggle of wolves over carrion, and thought that men of business could hardly be saved, for they lived by cheating and ruthless profiteering. It was monasticism, with its repudiation of the prizes and temptations of the secular way of life, which was, par excellence, the life of religion.[14] By contrast, the doctrine of original sin, the depravity of man, never had a foothold within the theology of the synagogue. It never held sway over the mind and the religious imagination of the Jews. In consequence of this, the body and the flesh were never regarded by them as contaminated, and the appetites and passions were not suspected of being rooted in evil.

The degree to which the ascetic temper of Christendom began to feel under threat from economic barbarism can

---

[14] See Tawney p.31

be assessed in terms of the severity of the measures aimed at protecting society from the usurious activity associated with the Jews. The fear of contagion from the purely contingent and temporal activity engaged in by this minority led to a strategy of exposing and isolating the threat. As early as 1179, the third Lateran Council banned usury and the legal status of Jews was made inferior to that of Christians in a number of areas including the possession of property. By 1215, not only did the Fourth Lateran Council, reiterate that Jews must not extract immoderate usury from Christians, but Jews were also to be distinguished as external to the body of believers by being compelled to dress differently from Christians, and wear a Jewish badge.

That the fear of the threat to the social organism never relaxed is demonstrated by the robustly defensive measures taken against usury in the Councils of Lyons (1274) and of Vienne (1312). At Lyons the strictures laid down by the third Lateran Council (1175) were not only reiterated, but strengthened by additional rules which made the money-lender an outlaw. The risks of infection were considered so great that anyone even so much as letting a house to a usurer would be excommunicated, foregoing their right to confession, absolution and Christian burial, and having their wills invalidated.

The further intensification of the defensive measures taken at the Council of Vienne is illustrative of the persistence of usury in Christian communities. A growing number of towns and regions sanctioned usury and compelled debtors to observe usurious contracts, in utter disregard for divine law. The threat of excommunication was used yet again against any rulers and magistrates knowingly maintaining such laws. The insidiousness of usury's growing grip on the body of Christendom also led the Council to order the opening of all money-lenders' accounts to ecclesiastical examination. Anyone who insisted that usury was not a sin would be dealt with by inquisitors as a heretic.

Even these stringencies were insufficient for Edward I of England who in 1290, at the height of the ecclesiastical measures against usury, took action to expel the Jews from his land. Many of them moved to France, only to face expulsion again in 1306 by King Philip IV, before settling in the future commercial centres of the Low Countries, especially Antwerp and Ghent.

It is true that the loosening of the leash on the economic dogs of modern-day materialism has not resulted in an unalloyed benefit to society. That which was once the servant, rather the master of civilisation, is now running wild to devastating effect. Regimented and nihilistic lives led to the rigid rule of economic expediency, so easily interpreted in terms of quantity, have overwhelmed any lingering folk memory of a rule of life superior to individual desires and temporary exigencies, which was what the medieval theorists meant by 'natural law.' It is hard to imagine the terror felt by medievals attempting to hold the economic wolves at bay, which only heightened their efforts to secure the integrity of the social organism as a complete whole. Their attempted defence against the encroachment of barbarism had in it something of the heroic, and to ignore the nobility of the war against usury is no less absurd than to idealise its practical results. The strength of the ascetic conviction, that was so viscerally opposed to the subordination of religion to economic interests, was demonstrated by the need for a similar persistence amongst the forces which would eventually overturn 'natural law' and desacralise society.

6 Our wills become one single will

An appreciation of the way in which the medieval mind strove for perfection undermines the modern demagogical condemnation of a herd-like mentality amongst individuals who lived in traditional societies. To suggest there was none of the sense of dignity and freedom of every individual, that only modern, 'evolved' mankind is supposed to have achieved, would be a gross distortion of the truth, resulting from a shallow analysis. Feudal peasants were rooted in the soil of their village communities generation after generation. This immobility, this enduring attachment to the soil, established a relationship between people and space. Being fixed in space led people to live in solitude and isolation. But the unit of isolation was not the individual, it was the group.

The majority of peasants lived grouped together in small villages. The division of labour required for agriculture was very simple, so it was unnecessary for many people to live together in the same place. Villages remained small and evenly distributed, the density being dictated by the productivity of the land. The isolated farm, a feature of the modern landscape, did not exist. Peasants lived grouped together for the following reasons. Firstly, the piece of land that each family cultivated was invariably small, typically divided into three strips of rotating crops, which were located with other family strips in an allocated field system. People lived together in the same place so that they could be close to the their fields. Secondly, where shared ownership and effort was required, such as ploughing and the use of oxen teams, people had to work together as a group, so living together was convenient. Thirdly, living together within a group also greatly contributed to everyone's security.

No matter what the reasons, and there are probably many more than those noted, the rural solitude was that of the group, not the individual. Because villagers did not move around much, the communities did not interact much. Life in a medieval village was very parochial as a result. Villagers restricted the scope of their daily activities: they did not travel far, they seldom made contact with the outside world, they led solitary lives, they maintained their own isolated social circle. The people they saw every day were the same people they had known since childhood, just as they knew the people in their own families. They did not have to select the kind of society they would live in, they were born into it, choice was not a factor.

In a society characterised by this level of familiarity, people achieved a level of freedom whereby they could do whatever they pleased without fear of violating the norms of the society. This type of freedom was different from the those freedoms in modern society, which are defined and regulated by laws. The social norms in a familiar society rested not upon laws but, rather, upon rituals and customs that were defined through practice; hence, to follow those norms was to follow one's own heart and mind. In other words, society and individual were one, a single social organism, a people of God, which aptly reflected St Paul's metaphor of the Church as the body of Christ.

We come back to the point that there was no division between the inner and personal life of religion, and the practical interests of the external order. Each individual in the western world, for example, was part of an order of faith that stretched from the parish church and manor, to kingship, the Holy Roman Empire and Christendom. The First Crusade, notable for not being merely a military operation, included vast numbers of ordinary men and women within a tide of humanity, known as the People's Crusade, that swept across Europe towards the Holy Land, probably representing the high water mark of medieval social cohesion from emperor to vassal. Such a coalition of souls could never have been imposed by the political or economic despotism of a centralised power. It grew from an acceptance that to comply perfectly with one's own specific function there was a need for an identical participation in the spirituality of the whole, conceived as a living organism. This kind of social order, with the sovereign at the centre, was the form within which the subjects demonstrated their faithfulness to God through faithfulness to their ruler. This faithfulness was a cornerstone of traditional society, in addition to work as rite and an elite that embodied transcendence. This was the force which as a magnet held together the social structure, establishing an implicit pull and gravitation between the individual and the centre, between the individual and the whole. It was a force acknowledged by Dante:

> *The essence of this blessed life consists*
> *in keeping to the boundaries of God's will,*
> *Through which our wills become one single will.*[15]

By contrast, modern society is composed of strangers. We fear that oral arrangements are not binding; therefore we draw up written contracts to which we sign our names. Laws arise in this fashion. But there was no way for laws like this to develop in feudal society, where trust was derived from familiarity.

Looked at this way, the decline of feudal society marked the decline of the personal freedom of familiarity and a separation of the inner and the outer selves. Few, save the king and officials, saw the need for any distinguishing signature or mark. Each signed with a cross just like everyone else, personal identity was not important or even understood. Perhaps it is not surprising that some of the early contractual agreements in the Middle Ages

---

[15] Dante, *Paradiso: Third Book of the Divine Comedy*, trans. A. Mandelbaum, University of California Press, New Jersey, 1984, Canto III ll. 79 - 81

were those drawn up with outsiders, in the form of money lending agreements. Notably, as one who was forced to live outside the community, a Jew would sign with a personal name.

There may not have been an absolute division in the medieval mind between the inner and personal life, which is the sphere of religion, and the practical interests of the external order, but there was a division of quality. The world of social organisation, originating in physical necessities, passed by insensible gradations into that of the spirit.

There was a gradation between nature and grace, between human appetites and religion. And what was true of the individual was true also of society. In the words of the famous Bull of Pope Boniface VIII: 'The way of religion is to lead the things which are lower to the things which are higher through the things which are intermediate. According to the law of the universe all things are not reduced to order equally and immediately; but the lowest through the intermediate, the intermediate through the higher'.[16] Thus social institutions assumed a character which may almost be called sacramental, for they were the outward and imperfect expression of a supreme spiritual reality. Ideally conceived, society was an organism of different grades, and human activities formed a hierarchy of functions, which differed in kind and in

---

[16] Quoted in Tawney, p.34

significance, but each of which was of value on its own plane, provided that it was governed, however remotely, by the end which is common to all. Like the celestial order, of which it was the dim reflection, society was stable because it was straining upwards across a Jacob's ladder connecting heaven and earth, in a cosmic harmony.

Thomas More's *Utopia*, written on the cusp of the medieval and modern worlds, was a self-conscious presentation of a rationally ordered state in which minds in harmony with Christ's teachings might exist. The money-free communal order was an echo of what had been lost. Utopia, governed by its ascetic spiritual discipline, was an image of man's soul aspiring to a state of redemption. The irony is that in the scholarly positing of this ideal from the outside, the humanist More was complicit in its final demise.

7 'Stand and do battle against Belial's children'

It all began with money, with the forces of usury circumventing, and later breaking, the religious prohibition of interest-taking. Then came commercial transactions in land, which struck a mortal blow against feudalism. Finally it was the turn of human labour, with man himself turned into a commodity by the slave trade and with the establishment of the wages system. The labour force, transformed into a commodity, became subject, like all others, to the laws of the market.

The common acceptance of the need to combat the relentless encroachments of usury upon the social organism, as demonstrated especially in the excommunicative strictures of the Council of Lyons (1274), marked the epitome of the medieval synthesis, a time when Europe was as close to being unified as it would ever be. And it was the papal role in calling the Council and others like it that demonstrated the role of the Christian Church in holding together a diverse, scattered, heterogeneous collection of people in a common citizenship, as a spiritual confraternity. The Church became responsible for education, art, literature, the care of the poor and the comfort of the dying. Immediately after the Council of Lyons, however, Christian unity was irredeemably shattered by political rivalries in which the Papacy itself was often a participant.

William Langland's poem *Piers the Ploughman* (written circa 1360–87) is the perfect expression of this decline with its sense of ruin, yet hope for rebirth should the right choices be made. The anguished protests of the poem ring out against the defeat of true Christianity by the spirit of hardened selfishness.

The dream landscape into which we are drawn by Langland furthers this idea of choice through symbolic imagery. The wilderness is the earth and the unknown dangers it entails. The tower on a 'toft' in the east is heaven; the deep dale and its dungeon are hell. These two put the poem in a cosmic perspective. What lies between the two extremes of heaven and hell is Langland's major concern: namely, the Field Full of Folk which represents the Christian community. The presence of heaven and hell reminds the reader that choices made during the brief and transitory life on earth have eternal consequences. One is challenged now to choose between heaven and hell.

The complete social spectrum is portrayed in the Field Full of Folk: the three estates, the rich and the poor, men and women. At once the element of choice appears. The people are 'werking and wandering as the world asketh'. Clearly the world's demand is interpreted in two different ways: there are those who work hard and obey the strictest dictates of their social position and estate, and there are those who selfishly accumulate material goods. Yet Langland is not being morally ambiguous, for the distinction between the right choice and the wrong choice is clear-cut. Hardworking ploughmen, anchorites and hermits who keep to their cells, and guiltless minstrels are the sort who are bound for heaven. The rest - gluttons, hermits in a heap, and friars, just to name a few - are the sort who are bound for hell. They have made the world and its pursuits their all. Notably, of those who have chosen worldliness, half are from the clerical estate. This spiritual rot undermines the Christian community that is portrayed in *Piers the Ploughman* and eventually causes its final collapse.

A believer in the Papacy, Langland deplored the failure of papal leadership and the Pope's growing encroachment on secular matters. Dante too was a devout Catholic who was a critic of the political ambitions of the Papacy, his great poem the culminating achievement of the medieval synthesis.

The popes of Langland's century had not been noted religious reformers but, rather, preoccupied with the secular concerns of law, statesmanship and questions of empire; activities which eventually cost the Papacy religious credibility. As a result, Dante gave his support to the Holy Roman Emperor against the Pope, with the vision of the radical Spiritual Franciscans and the apocalyptic followers of Joachim of Flora influencing his political writings, rather than the heavily modified Aristotelianism of Thomas Aquinas. The defeated Pope Boniface acquiesced in the victory of Philip IV of France, which marked the triumph of the temporal over the spiritual power.

The Avignon Papacy itself grew in efficiency and political skill, but as it did, lost still more spiritual prestige, and religious reformers looked increasingly to the state for an implementation of their ideas. William of Ockham, for example, the most important thinker of the age, allied himself with the Emperor against the Pope. State-Papacy conflicts, as exemplified by Philip and Boniface, would not be reconciled. Fifteenth-century Conciliarism, which was founded on the principle that the universal church was a congregation of the faithful, not the Roman Church, was the last great struggle to preserve medieval unity on some basis other than the Papacy.

William Langland wrote, 'He called that house Unity - which is Holy Church in English'. Yet no one was more aware than Langland of the crumbling Christian edifice. The whole of *Piers the Ploughman* is an impassioned plea for social and religious reform, so much so that he has sometimes been regarded as a harbinger of the Protestant Reformation. But his emphasis was always on a forlorn call to unity: 'Call we to all the Commons that they come into Unity and there stand and do battle against Belial's children.'

Until Langland's time, markets had played a subordinate, local role, hemmed in by the limited economic boundaries of the feudal world. Human beings, land and money were not subject to the laws of the market. Non-economic norms set by the political and religious hierarchies regulated human labour and the ownership of land, neither of which were commercially transferable. 'Belial's children' however, would not be held at bay. Though trafficking in money was notionally blocked by the religious prohibition of usury, it continued to be carried out in increasing volumes by those excluded from feudal society, forced to live on its margins or in its pores. The money germ would not be dislodged and eventually it would eat away Christendom.

8 Martin Luther and the new paideuma

'The Catholic Church went out of business when its hierarchy ceased to believe its own dogma. Leo X didn't take Luther's thought as a serious matter. He didn't expect others to do so.'[17] So wrote Ezra Pound on the Reformation. If the misuse of money was seen by the medieval church as the major threat to the social unity of Christendom, imagine the despair of the faithful when the Pope himself resorted to financial chicanery to finance the renovation of St Peter's Basilica in Rome.

The banker known as Jakob Fugger the Rich was chosen by Pope Leo X to manage the money-raising campaign. Johanne Tetzel, a Dominican friar and preacher, began the sale of indulgences across the German lands. In particular, Albert, the Archbishop of Maintz, agreed to allow the sale of the indulgences in his territory in exchange for a cut of the proceeds. He did so in order to pay off the debts he had incurred in paying for his high church rank.

Despairing of the money corruption and usury-driven indulgences, Martin Luther famously nailed his ninety five

---

[17] E. Pound, *Guide to Kulchur*, New Directions, New York, 1970, p.75

theses to the door of Wittenberg cathedral in 1517. Within two weeks, copies of the Theses had spread throughout Germany; within two months throughout Europe.

Though more and more commonplace in the late medieval period, usury was still considered a sin and one most closely associated with the Jews. So when in 1520 Luther wrote in his letter *To the Christian Nobility of the Christian Nations,* that 'Fugger and similar people really need to be kept in check', he was speaking against the usurious activities of bankers and Jews, with convictions that were consistent with those that had driven in the nails at Wittenberg three years earlier. Luther's intention had been to cleanse the church of its money corruption and return it to a simple theology of the cross. Unintentionally, he had unleashed the great forces of the Reformation, the reverberations of which can still be felt in our own times.

It is possible to imagine a Luther without a Calvin, but hardly conceivable to imagine a Calvin without a Luther. Nevertheless, once Luther had opened up the doors to reform, Calvin rushed in to rearrange the ecclesiastical furniture. In his fear of the sacrilegious and socially corrupting power of money, Luther remained socially conservative, whereas the second generation reformer, John Calvin, was a force for radicalism. Calvin assumed an economic organisation that was relatively advanced as far as the power of money and trade was concerned, and expounded a social ethics on the basis of the seemingly inevitable future. Thus John Calvin stood in marked contrast to Luther and the medieval theologians who proceeded him.

The medieval church had striven to keep the uses of money limited and under control, with usury in the most widely defined sense outlawed as an excommunicable offence. Society was conceived holistically as a people of God, which reflected St Paul's metaphor of the Church as the body of Christ. In this social organism the parts, though varied, each carried out vital functions for the survival of the whole. Disproportionate growth of any one part, such as trade for monetary gain, was seen as a malignant threat to the rest, quite apart from the biblical admonishment of usury as sinful.

Calvinism, an urban movement, found its stronghold in social groups to which the traditional scheme of social ethics had become irrelevant. Its most influential adherents operated in the great business centres such as Antwerp and Ghent with their industrial hinterland, London and Amsterdam, strongly influenced by generations of Jewish emigres whose antecedents had been ousted from Spain, France and England. For any reformed theology to thrive in these new conditions, it had to start from a frank recognition of the necessity of capital, credit and banking. That is just what Calvinism did, by breaking with the tradition that regarded a preoccupation with economic interests beyond the needs of subsistence as sinful, and which stigmatised the middle-man as a parasite and the usurer as a thief.

Under the new and progressive urban conditions, the rules were turned upon their head. Whereas to strive for personal enrichment had once seemed incomprehensible, for the Calvinist there was nothing wrong with good honest profit, as he understood it, derived from diligence and industry. Usury became respectable, where it has previously been condemned as immoral. Calvin and his followers assumed credit to be a normal fact of life; and the financier was not a pariah, but a useful member of society.

Luther believed that anyone could reach salvation as long as he had faith. In the 1538 edition of his commentary on Galatians, Luther spoke of 'this one and firm rock, which we call the doctrine of justification, that is, that we are delivered from sin, death, and devil, not through ourselves (nor certainly through our works which are of lesser value than we ourselves), but through outside help, through the Only-begotten Son of God, Jesus Christ.' 'If the article concerning justification falls, everything falls.'[18] In contrast, Calvin preached that those predestined for salvation were defined by their virtuous lives, and they were referred to as 'the elect'. Furthermore, the elect could be determined by their economic and material success. Under this doctrine, good works, whilst not a way of

---

[18] Quoted by H. J. A. Bouman, 'The Doctrine of Justification in the Lutheran Confessions', *Concordia Theological Monthly,* Vol. 26, No.11, November 1955, p.801

attaining salvation, become indispensable as a proof that salvation has been attained.

The aptitudes cultivated by a life devoted to business found their complement in the new theology, which formed the basis of a new paideuma, a term coined by Leo Frobenius and described by Ezra Pound as meaning 'the tangle or complex of the inrooted ideas of any period. . . , the gristly roots of ideas that are in action'.[19] In this Reformation paideuma of the Calvinists, the will of God was allied with the economic virtues that had escaped the clutches of the restrictive traditional belief system of the medieval Roman church. The escapees and inverters of the values of tradition from this point would see all forms of traditional belief as barriers in the path of progress; and it would be a linear path into the future, in keeping with Judaic tradition. Calvin's emphasis on Sola Scriptura, meaning the Scriptures as a unique revelation of the way to life, threw a much greater emphasis upon the *Old Testament* for the individual Christian than under the Roman Catholic tradition. With the stories from the Hebrew *Bible* as their example, all opposition from tradition along the path ahead would be dealt with as ruthlessly as Joshua dealt with Jericho. In their determination to clear the pathway ahead, the adherents of the new paideuma would use every weapon at their disposal, including subterfuge, political revolution and war, because the issue at stake was not perceived to be merely economic self-

---

[19] Pound, pp.57-8

interest, but now the will of God, later to be the will of the people. Society would now consist of the elect and unelect, winners and losers, the chosen and the rest, in a civil society that grew out of Calvin's covenantal, or contractual, view of church and society as voluntary associations.

Medieval society had been characterised by familiarity; people achieved a level of freedom whereby they could do whatever they pleased without fear of violating the norms of the society. After the Reformation, civil society would slowly, but surely, sever all the ties of familiarity, put egoism and selfish need in the place of familial ties, and dissolve the human world into one of atomistic individuals who are inimically opposed to one another. Man's supreme relation became the legal one. His relation to laws became valid for him not because they were the familiar laws of his own will and nature, but because they were the dominant man-made laws and because departure from them was avenged by the law-makers.

There had once been no division between the inner and personal life of religion and the practical interests of the external order. After the Reformation all national, natural, moral, and theoretical conditions would become extrinsic to man. Practical need and egoism began to replace salvation as the motivating force of society and, as such, would eventually appear in purest form as soon as civil society had fully given birth to the political states of Western Europe and North America. Undoubtedly, in the new monotheism following the Reformation, money became and remains the god of practical need and self-interest. The rending of the inner life from the external material world continues to this day, as the dominant economies with their liberal ideology, have countenanced no resistance to the imposition of civil society and the worship of money worldwide.

By 1571 in England, a mere thirty years after the suppression of the monasteries, the Act of 1552, which had prohibited all interest as 'a vyce moste odyous and detestable, as in dyvers places of the hollie Scripture it is evident to be seen',[20] had been swept away. This was but a manifestation of the new paideuma, which held that the world of money and commerce existed in an amoral sphere of their own, separate and apart from religion and ethics.

Religious belief would become increasingly a private affair, whilst the 'freedom' of the market reflected the struggle amongst the various possessors of wealth for supremacy. Everything would have its price in this blind battle of everyone against everyone. Everything would eventually be bought and sold. Nothing would escape the meshes of this devil's mill. Gone was the concept of society as a social organism in which everyone had his or her diverse, but equally important part to play.

There had been no place in Christian medieval life for any economic activity which was unrelated to a sacred

---

[20] Quoted in Tawny, p.183

end. It is important to understand the holistic nature of this worldview, for it was the totality of traditional society that distinguished it from the post-Reformation world, in which work came to be accepted as a practical necessity, a view that would eventually fragment tradition's authority. In fact, fragmentation could be said to be the hallmark of the new paideuma.

Luther did not live to see anything even approximating to the full fruition of the social change wrought by his actions. He was aware, however, of the direction of travel and, as can be seen in his later writings, it left him in despair. Having given full vent to his anger against the sale of indulgences by the Catholic Church, he lived to see the forces of the Reformation leading to the very acceptance of the usurious practices that he warned must be kept in check. Society had turned in the very opposite direction to that which he had intended in his criticism of the Church's financial malpractices. The banking culture emanating from commercial centres such as Antwerp and Ghent could not be associated solely with the Jews. After all, the Pope's banker, Fugger the Rich, the most successful banker of his day, was a Catholic. However, the myriad of accusations that Luther levelled against the Jews, most notably in *On the Jews and Their Lies*, demonstrate that he associated the lending of money for interest with a Judaic frame of mind, the influence of which had long since broken free of the restrictions laid down by the great Councils of Lyons and Vienne. Of the Jews Luther wrote:

...they are nothing but thieves and robbers who daily eat no morsel and wear no thread of clothing which they have not stolen and pilfered from us by means of their accursed usury. Thus they live from day to day, together with wife and child, by theft and robbery, as arch-thieves and robbers, in the most impenitent security.[21]

Many commentators have attempted to separate these railings of the older Luther from the young reforming radical before the great cathedral door of Wittenberg. However, Luther's contempt for usury was consistent throughout his life. The harshness of tone in his old age simply reflected the increased despair at the pace of the revolution in social attitudes that was taking place before his very eyes.

In his sermons, Luther preached against covenantal Christianity, advocating instead the theology of the cross.

This difference between the Law and the Gospel is the height of knowledge in Christendom. Every person and all persons who assume or glory in the name of Christian should know and be able to state this difference. If this ability is lacking, one cannot tell a Christian from a heathen or a Jew; of such supreme

---

[21] Quoted in M. Perry, *Sources of the Western Tradition: Volume I: From Ancient Times to the Enlightenment*, Wadsworth Cenage Learning, Boston, 2014, p.339

importance is this differentiation. This is why St.
Paul so strongly insists on a clean-cut and proper
differentiating of these two doctrines.
(Martin Luther, *Sermon on Galatians*, 1532)

He must have seen, however, that a return to the Law was taking hold in early post-Reformation Europe and he would have interpreted this movement with dread. He knew that in the early days of the church the unbelieving mind had interpreted the cross as nonsense. A religion founded on the crushing, filthy death of a man cursed by God was foolishness to Greeks and an offence to Jews, depending on whether their sin was intellectual arrogance or moralistic self-righteousness. In the theological turn taken, soon to be full-blown Calvinism, Luther could see the same rejection of the cross and cycle of sin repeated.

As Luther saw it, the living Word of God in Christ ceased to be a restraint upon economic self-interest. The Law of the *Old Testament* had instead become allied with the self-righteous economic virtues of the age as a reason why self-interest should be given free play, an attitude that would later be systematised economically by Adam Smith and philosophically by John Locke. The same values that led Luther to condemn the financial chicanery of Leo X were those that left him exasperated at the new paideuma or, as Luther would have understood it, the Judaic paiduema that was taking hold.

9 What is truth?

Luther's rhetoric of antithesis contrasted the destructive force, which he clearly associated with money, usury and a reversion to the Law on the one hand, and a theology of the cross on the other. He associated the first of these antithetical states with the disordered and fragmented nature of fallen man. Whilst in the latter, he valued the hierarchical harmony of the natural order - the truth no less.

In the modern world, we have come to think about sin in a subjective way and have completely lost sight of the objectivity with which it was once understood. The medieval mind felt itself sufficiently in touch with objective truth to know that sin was a disruption of the objective nature of things, the natural order. It was a blindness to the truth.

This cast of mind defined original justice as order and original sin as disorder, or a rebellion against the cosmic hierarchy. It was vertical in orientation and in accord with the way of religion that 'is to lead the things which are lower to the things which are higher, through the things which are intermediate.'[22] Social institutions assumed a sacramental character as the outward and imperfect expression of a supreme spiritual reality, in which the

---

[22] The Bull of Pope Boniface VIII, quoted in Tawney, p.34

forces of destruction and disorder were held at bay. Society itself was conceived as a single organism, a people of God, which lived out St Paul's metaphor of the Church as the body of Christ.

The social organism was founded on the principle of unity in multiplicity. Each thing was considered to be in a relationship with something else in conformity with their respective natures, and thus in conformity with the right to fulfil those natures.

Hierarchy in the social organism was accepted as an extension of the cosmic harmony, without which a reversion to the fallen state of man would ensue. Without hierarchy there would be disorder; the realisation of a particular nature would clash with all other natures seeking egotistic fulfilment.

This contrasts with modern thought, in which an individual right is always absolute and therefore excludes all others. Any attempt to give all rights equal validity fails, because equality destroys rights, i.e. the right of a nature to be what it is. Equality is eventually reached on a commodity basis, on the purely quantitative plane of numerical unities ($1 = 1$), which is only possible through the destruction of all the qualitative differences that make up these diverse natures. Equality destroys diversity and a right ends up being the right to nothing.

In the medieval social organism, it was accepted that hierarchy was needed to preserve this right, which must renounce its absoluteness and consent to its own relativity. One right would have more of a right to something than another; but this renunciation was not felt as resignation and compromise, it was based on something other than constraint. There was no police enforcement of the law in medieval society. The hierarchical subordination of individuals in the social organism required the submission of the creature to the Creator, the relative to the Absolute. By this act of submission, all natures had access to a formal and qualitative equality, not horizontally amongst themselves, but vertically with regard to God.

A refusal to submit would be tantamount to repeating the Fall, the act of revolt that had repercussions all along the hierarchical axis. The natures forming this axis were not destroyed by that act of original sin, but they could no longer fulfil themselves according to their truth. They had no role in a structure. They were like the stones of a toppled building scattered on the ground, become horizontal, but with the pattern of the vertical hierarchy remaining to those who would but see it. By Adam's sin 'original justice was taken away, whereby not only were the lower powers of the soul held together under the control of reason, without any disorder whatsoever, but the whole body was held together in subjection to the soul, without any defect.' (St Thomas)

The destruction of original justice had resulted in a new order. In reality this was a disorder but, and this is the critical point, it was not self-apparent, precisely because there was no longer any access to the criteria of the original hierarchy, which alone could reveal it to be a disorder. This meant that the disorder was lived as order. Adam could not have known the truth of sin. Moreover, it is not by chance that the dogma of original sin was not elaborated in the Old Testament, but by St Paul. As if to emphasise this great unknowing, Christ repeatedly exposed the Pharisaical adherence to the Law of his detractors as sinful self-righteousness. The point made was that no-one could understand what happened on the last day of earthly Paradise until the day of Christ's passion. In Jean Borella's words, 'we needed to wait for the Incarnation of that One who is Truth, infinite Wisdom, Sun of Justice, Hypostatic Hierarchy, the Divine Word, for the injustice of sin to be fully and totally revealed'.[23]

The Pharisaic followers of the Law handed Christ over to that epitome of worldly pragmatism, Pontius Pilate. In the Passion, therefore, Christ confronted all that was contemptible in the state of fallen man: self-righteousness and pragmatism. To Pilate's question 'so you are a king?' Jesus answered 'you say I am a king. For this I was born, and for this I have come into the world, to bear witness to the truth...' The pragmatic Pilate responds with the question 'What is truth?'

Subjectivism and moral relativism are betrayed in the very question. They were prominent in the very self-

---

[23] J. Borella, *The Secret of the Christian Way*, State University of New York Press, New York, 2001, p.101 (My underline)

righteousness of the Jews who, together with Pilate, spurned the truth in condemning Christ. They remain prominent also in the liberalism of the present, which has also rejected the truth of the cross. The truth in all its grandeur and purity was not apparent before the raising of Christ on the cross. From that point, the world could only be true to the extent that it reflected God, the creative logic and the eternal reason that brought it into being. For with Christ's passion a new hierarchy came into being that united man to other men in their union with God, through Christ. If the truth is objective, then 'bearing witness to the truth' means giving priority to God and his will - the truth of the cosmic hierarchy - over against the interests of this world and its powers. The antithesis stated in these terms could not be more stark - choose God or the devil.

We have seen that medieval society sought to reflect the truth in an order of faith that stretched from the parish church and manor, to kingship, the Holy Roman Empire and Christendom. Securing the resultant social organism meant the maintenance of a constant vigilance against forces that were wholly inimicable to Christic justice, namely the Muslim threat externally and the practice of usury internally.

No wonder the increased acceptance of usury and a reversion to the Law in theology was met with so much hostility by Luther. Calvinistic covenantal theology was for him a replaying of the Fall.

10 From out of Ghent: disorder given legitimacy

If Luther saw the cosmic hierarchy come crashing down as a toppled building, leaving men to live amongst the ruins, then the cracks that would eventually cause the edifice to crumble were already beginning to widen 300 years before. If a replaying of the Fall began with money, then the earliest cracks in the edifice would have been in the neighbouring commercial centres of Antwerp and Ghent, and their hinterlands of Amsterdam and London. In commerce, man is not defined by his place in the cosmic order, his status is defined by wealth. Out of this deviation from the order would emerge thinking to legitimise the resultant disorder.

Ghent became an important trading centre in the 11th and 12th centuries, thanks to the local production of cloth, made from imported English wool. The scholastic philosopher known as Henry of Ghent (1217 - 1293) was born and lived in the city at this time. He was one of a number of scholastics concerned with the issue that philosophers described as univocity, the question of whether one can speak univocally, in the same terms, when describing the attributes of God and man. Henry believed that the divide between God and man was so great that it was impossible to say, for example, that God is good. This was a philosophical development of colossal importance. If one could not say that God is good, that meant that God was absolutely transcendent and man was sitting here on earth by himself. This development was not atheism; God was there after all, He created the universe. He may be good or benign, but we cannot say or know for sure. With Henry of Ghent, the world suddenly became very flat. There was a shift from a world that was vertical, where man was a participant in the higher order, to a world that was horizontalised. After all, if you could no longer describe God, if knowledge of God was not accessible to man and the higher order was too transcendent, then one was left to talk about the things of which we have knowledge. Man was left to focus his attention upon the things of this world.

The idea of a special connection between the thought of John Duns Scotus (1266–1308) and that of his forebear, Henry of Ghent, goes back to the time of Duns himself.[24] In the full knowledge of this connection, and knowing too Henry of Ghent's idea that man is unhooked from the higher order, it is hardly surprising that both Henry of Ghent and Duns Scotus were predominantly voluntarist

---

[24] S.P. Marron, 'Henry of Ghent and Duns Scotus on the Knowledge of Being', *Speculum*, The Medieval Academy of America, Cambridge, Massachusetts, Vol 63, No 1, Jan, 1988, pp. 22-57

in their philosophical outlook, believing the will to be a greater power than the intellect. From a different starting point, the intellectualist position, St Thomas Aquinas would come to the same judgement. Unlike an animal, which acts upon instinct, 'man acts from judgment, because by his apprehensive power he judges that something should be avoided or sought. But because this judgment, in the case of some particular act, is not from a natural instinct, but from some act of comparison in the reason, therefore he acts from free judgment and retains the power of being inclined to various things'.[25]

The result of this disconnection of man's will from the divine was that it became increasingly implausible to think politically from the position of the general good. The concept of the general good, as it was understood previously by the medieval mind and prior to that, by the Greeks and Romans, was founded upon the principle of a natural order, a cosmic harmony, and the freedom to do the right thing, which meant hierarchical subordination within the social organism. However, if freedom becomes what the individual determines it to be, then political action can no longer be an assertion of some common understanding of the general good, but has to be, instead, about rights. A very different political life was about to

---

[25] St. Thomas Aquinas, *Summa Theologica*, Question 83, Article 1, trans. Fathers of the English Dominican Province, Christian Classics Etherial Library, Calvin College, Michigan, p.931, online resource http://www.ccel.org/ccel/aquinas/summa.pdf , citation dated 6.2.14

emerge that was founded upon the protection of individual rights. This embryonic individualism takes us back to the new commercial centres, like Ghent, where money had become the new arbiter of power; except that now the deviation from the cosmic order, the disorder, had been given the philosophical and political legitimacy to be lived as the new order.

11 A world desacralised

It has already been noted how the pursuit of individual rights would eventually lead to a destruction of diversity in the drive to achieve the numerical unities of 1=1. The same homogenising impact was felt upon man's appreciation of time, which became desacralised and rendered indifferent to notions of natural order and hierarchy. Throughout the Middle Ages the liturgical year, to most people quite simply the year, was spangled with religious festivities and with days marked by sacred events. 'The whole of social life developed within the seasons of prayer, and the meaning of these was to remind Christians that their life took place within salvation history. Though the name 'liturgical' year is much later than the Middle Ages, it owes the essentials of its organisation to a time before the Middle Ages, with the temporal on the one hand and the sanctoral on the other'.[26]

Here indeed was the residue of pagan cyclic time, which the missionary monks who evangelised Northern Europe adapted to their own ends. They noted how the natural

---

[26] *Encyclopedia of the Middle Ages*, ed. A. Vauchez, R. Barrie Dobson, M. Lapidge, James Clarke and Co, Cambridge, 2000, p.857.

season of Spring coincided with the Christian season of catechesis and penance leading to Easter, with the result that it became known among Anglo-Saxon people simply as 'Lenthen', 'Spring'. This is the source of our English word 'Lent'. Lent is a spiritual Springtime of growth and new life. Another example was the way the date of Christ's birth apparently replaced the pagan celebration of the Winter solstice, December 25th.[27] For the people whose pagan rituals had been Christianised, time was not a linear, 'historical' time. Time and becoming were related to what is superior to time; in this way the perception of time underwent a spiritual transformation.

However, an extension of the money-based rule of quantity reduced pagan concepts of time to a memory held in the names of the months and the days of the week. With the dominance of money came the final victory of Judaic linear chronology, a current of thought introduced into the mainstream of Christian thinking by St Augustine in *The City of God*. With the stripping of the altars in the Reformation went the stripping of the year of its festivals and saints days. Time became ruthlessly linear with an indifference to its contents; a simple irreversible order of consecutive events, its parts mutually homogeneous and therefore measurable in a quantitative fashion. The emphasis from now would be upon progression, and woe betide anyone who might step into the path of progress.

---

[27] P. Elliott, *Ceremonies of the Liturgical Year: According to the Modern Roman Rite,* Ignatius Press, San Francisco, 2002, p.2

Man's very appreciation of the space around him suffered a similar diminution and homogenisation. In antiquity, as Evola described, every direction corresponded to given influences, out of which, for example, came 'the doctrine of the sacred orientations in the arrangement of the temples'. This continued into the Christian era in 'the art of the orientation of the cathedrals that was preserved in Europe up to the Middle Ages'.[28] There were, of course, degrees of sacredness even within the consecrated buildings themselves, which were wholly dependent on spacial arrangements and location.

A sacred geography inspired lands and cities as the centres of spiritual influence on earth: special places of pilgrimage, where man could be closer to God. Such thinking was expressed in the celebrated Mappa Mundi of Hereford Cathedral, which has Jerusalem at its centre, from which other lands radiate. It is a map of sacred, rather than mere physical geography.

However, a money-based rule of quantity ensured that man's experience of space became just as desacralised as time, being equally indifferent to its contents. Space became perceived as a 'simple container of bodies and motions, totally indifferent to both'.[29] There was an assumption of homogeneity. A particular area of space became 'the objective equivalent of another one, and the

---

[28] Evola, p.150

[29] Evola, p.148

fact that a thing is found - or that an event may take place - in one point of space rather than in another, does not confer any particular quality to the intimate nature of that thing or of that event'.[30]

The Middle Ages also respected a traditional concept of land under conditions that reflected a vertically orientated order. Ownership could not be conceived as other than a sacred privilege, which implied a commitment on the part of the feudal lord to be faithful to his prince, by upholding religious as well as a political and military values. This fides represented a readiness to die and offer self-sacrifice in the cause of the social organism, in a way that overcame individual interests in a well-developed ethics of honour. To own, to be lord of a land was a spiritual and not merely a political title and commitment.

However, a fundamental shift in the psychology of land-ownership went hand-in-hand with the desacralisation of time and space. All notions of obligation to the social organism withered away as quickly as the religious prohibitions on usury began to crumble. This was most clearly demonstrated in the land clearances of the English countryside from the late Middle Ages, due to the expansion of the woollen industry and the economic expediency of replacing people with sheep.

---

[30] Evola, p.148

Taking the typical landowner of the time as his example, Tawney captured the change in mood.

The official opposition to depopulation, which had begun in 1489 and was to last almost until 1640, infuriated him as an intolerable interference with the rights of property. In their attacks on the restraints imposed by village custom below and by the crown from the above, in their illegal defiance of the statutes forbidding depopulation, and in their fierce resistance to the attempts of Wolsey and Somerset to restore the old order, the interests which were making the agrarian revolution were watering the seeds of that individualistic conception of ownership which was to carry all before it after the civil war.

Once the individualistic doctrine was accepted...

...it was to silence the preaching of all social duties save that of submission. If property be an unconditional right, emphasis on its obligations is little more than the graceful parade of a flattering, but innocuous, metaphor. For, whether the obligations are fulfilled or neglected, the right continues unchallenged and indefeasible,...[31]

In the covenantal post-Reformation era, legal rights were extended, whilst obligations founded upon familiarity were repudiated. A new ideology of irresponsible ownership

---

[31] Tawney, p.152

became the hallmark of the new order, resulting from the same apparition of the 'will' that emerged to light with Henry of Ghent, Duns Scotus and Thomas Aquinas. The breaking up of property, separating it from the rigorous norms of the paternal right and primogeniture, manifested the degeneration of the traditional spirit and departure from the natural order. Evola described this as an act of desecration.

> *The land, which may also belong to a merchant... or to a serf, is a desecrated land: in conformity with the interests typical of the two inferior castes, which have succeeded in taking the land away from the ancient type of 'feudal lords', the land is only valued from an economic point of view and it is exploited as much as possible with machines and other modern technical devices.*[32]

Under disorder lived as order, both lord and serf were 'freed' from their respective obligations to the social organism. From this point on, one would be seeking the highest price for land, the other would want the highest price for labour. To the one, land ownership no longer brought with it obligations; rather it had become a financial asset. To the other, work was no longer a rite; rather it had become a practical necessity. The separation of blood from the soil left all strata of society with a subjectivist pathos before nature. The poetic and subjective impressions

---

[32] Evola, p.156

typical of a romantic soul are something new. Before these times, man had real sensations of the world around him.

In a life of obligation within the social organism, life itself was religion, not simply something to which one deferred on a Sunday. The experience of the world was immediate, often demanding symbolical representation 'as gods, demons, elementals, and spirits ruling over places and phenomena'.[33] And these symbols were not arbitrary acts of the imagination. Just as the pressure of the blankets might give rise to the image of a falling rock in a dream, then an ordinary waking experience of the world gave rise to symbolic representations that arose out of necessity, as integrations with the world that did not occur casually. The subject and predicate were opposite to our own. Truth was the self-disclosure to man of the things around him. All man did was represent the truth symbolically.

Under life lived as order, man did not stand back from the world and observe it, he was totally engaged and immersed in a hyper-realism. How unlike the man 'freed' from social obligation who, separated from the world in a state of subjectivist pathos, would be condemned to understand the world from a distance; thus science and art would adopt the characteristics of the disorder lived as order, setting an academic seal of approval upon a fallen world, the chief characteristics of which would be:

---

[33] Evola, p.151

71

- The apparition of free will
- Belief in a unilinear history, evolutionism and progressivism
- Priority to quantity, not quality, and the commodification of everything, including human life
- The desacralisation of land
- Individualism and 'freedom' from social obligation
- Subjectivism and a distancing from reality

Have we not already noted, how in the modern world, we have come to think about sin in a subjective way and have completely lost sight of the objectivity with which it was once understood?

12 'Mundane principles' in the ascendancy

The essential ingredients of a civil society, so feared by Luther as a new judaic paideuma, were openly affirmed as such by Karl Marx.

When Marx wrote of Christianity, he was expressing his thoughts on the full-blown Calvinistic, covenantal view of church and society as voluntary associations, which would eventually come to be accepted by all the denominations of the faith, openly or tacitly. Religion was no longer a life to be lived, but a private belief to be entered into voluntarily and practiced privately, outside of the economic sphere. Meanwhile, in this economic sphere, or civil society, Marx described how life was led in the 'spirit' of Judaism, by <u>all</u>.

> *Judaism has held its own alongside Christianity, not only as religious criticism of Christianity, not only as the embodiment of doubt in the religious derivation of Christianity, but equally because the practical-Jewish spirit, Judaism, has maintained itself and even attained its highest development in*

Christian society. The Jew, who exists as a distinct member of civil society, is only a particular manifestation of the Judaism of civil society.[34]

From being the despised values of a persecuted minority, which doggedly persisted in its pursuit of economic gain against the strictures of the Councils of Lyons and Vienne, the source of disorder that brought down the vertical hierarchy of Christendom, the commercialism associated with the Jews, had become accepted as the new order. Marx asked, 'what, in itself, was the basis of the Jewish religion?' He answered: 'practical need, egoism'.[35]

The monotheism of the Jew, therefore, is in reality the polytheism of the many needs, a polytheism which makes even the lavatory an object of divine law. Practical need, egoism, is the principle of civil society, and as such appears in pure form as soon as civil society has fully given birth to the political state. The god of practical need and self-interest is money.

Money is the jealous god of Israel, in face of which no other god may exist. Money degrades all the gods of man – and turns them into commodities. Money is the universal self-established value of all things. It has therefore robbed the whole world – both

---

[34] K. Marx, *On the Jewish Question, Marx and Engels Collected Works,* Vol. 3, 1975, Lawrence and Wishart, London, p.171

[35] Marx, *Jewish Question,* p.171

the world of men and nature – of its specific value. Money is the estranged essence of man's work and man's existence, and this alien essence dominates him, and he worships it.[36]

Man had exchanged the God of heaven for the 'god of the world', Mammon. Under no account whatsoever is the historical development in this era to be seen as a progression to a new and enlightened modernity; that would be falling into the trap of believing the victor's history and philosophy. Man exchanged one belief for another: one based on the vision of attaining as close an alignment as possible to the cosmic order, the other based on money. Marx, writing 300 years later than Luther, recognised as an established fact that which Luther could see coming: money had become the foundation of the new secular order. Judaism was the metaphorical expression used by Marx for that which was now espoused by all.

The god of the Jews has become secularised and has become the god of the world. The bill of exchange is the real god of the Jew. His god is only an illusory bill of exchange.[37]

The worship of money now separated all men from reality, leaving nature to be a thing of dreams and pathos.

---

[36] Marx, *Jewish Question*, p.172

[37] Marx, *Jewish Question*, p.172

The view of nature attained under the dominion of private property and money is a real contempt for and practical debasement of nature; in the Jewish religion nature exists, it is true, but it exists only in imagination.[38]

There is a price for everything.

It is in this sense that Thomas Münzer declares it intolerable 'that all creatures have been turned into property, the fishes in the water, the birds in the air, the plants on the earth; the creatures, too, must become free'.[39]

A virtue is made of stripping all the values out of life, except the monetary ones.

Contempt for theory, art, history, and for man as an end in himself, which is contained in an abstract form in the Jewish religion, is the real, conscious standpoint, the virtue of the man of money. The species-relation itself, the relation between man and woman, etc., becomes an object of trade! The woman is bought and sold.[40]

---

[38] Marx, *Jewish Question,* p.172

[39] Marx, *Jewish Question,* p.172

[40] Marx, *Jewish Question,* p.172

National identity and all diversity are lost.

> *The chimerical nationality of the Jew is the nationality of the merchant, of the man of money in general.*[41]

The new morality neither looks up to the divine, nor is it grounded in anything.

> *The groundless law of the Jew is only a religious caricature of groundless morality and right in general, of the purely formal rites with which the world of self-interest surrounds itself.*[42]

In the breakdown of the ties of familiarity and non-monetary relationships, all ties become contractual.

> *Here, too, man's supreme relation is the legal one, his relation to laws that are valid for him not because they are laws of his own will and nature, but because they are the dominant laws and because departure from them is avenged.*[43]

And yet, the money-makers can break these laws with impunity, sowing the seeds of distrust.

---

[41] Marx, *Jewish Question*, p.172

[42] Marx, *Jewish Question*, p.172

[43] Marx, *Jewish Question*, p.172

Jewish Jesuitism, the same practical Jesuitism which Bauer discovers in the Talmud, is the relation of the world of self-interest to the laws governing that world, the chief art of which consists in the cunning circumvention of these laws.

Indeed, the movement of this world within its framework of laws is bound to be a continual suspension of law.[44]

Life as religion and work as rite had been superseded by the actions of practical necessity.

Judaism could not develop further as a religion, could not develop further theoretically, because the world outlook of practical need is essentially limited and is completed in a few strokes.

By its very nature, the religion of practical need could find its consummation not in theory, but only in practice, precisely because its truth is practice.[45]

There had been a fundamental shift from a social organism that was founded on the principle of unity in multiplicity to one in which qualitative differences were eroded within a fragmenting society.

---

[44] Marx, *Jewish Question*, p.172-3

[45] Marx, *Jewish Question*, p.173

Judaism reaches its highest point with the perfection of civil society, but it is only in the Christian world that civil society attains perfection. Only under the dominance of Christianity, which makes all national, natural, moral, and theoretical conditions extrinsic to man, could civil society separate itself completely from the life of the state, sever all the species-ties of man, put egoism and selfish need in the place of these species-ties, and dissolve the human world into a world of atomistic individuals who are inimically opposed to one another.

Christianity sprang from Judaism. It has merged again in Judaism.[46]

It is to this extent that, within the metaphorical parameters of Marx's critique, the dominant western culture became Judaic. Marx's own summarised evaluation of this most profound cultural shift was selected by Julian Evola for inclusion in *Revolt Against the Modern World*, for the terse way that it captured the major turning point in western thought.

What are the mundane principles of Judaism? Practical necessity and the pursuit of one's own advantage. What is its earthly god? Money. The Jew has emancipated himself in a typically Jewish fashion not only in that he has taken control of the

---

[46] Marx, *Jewish Question*, p.173

power of money, but also in that through him, money has become a world power and the practical Jewish spirit has become the spirit of the Christian people. The Jews have emancipated themselves insofar as the Christians have become Jews. The god of the Jews has become secularised and has become the god of the earth. The exchange is the true god of the Jews.[47]

The antithesis between these 'mundane principles of Judaism' (driven by economic and monetary goals) and a declining tradition founded on a divine principle, however the latter might manifest itself in different cultures, has been the principle point of conflict in world history, rendering other political differences quite minor. It is the antithesis at the heart of any meaningful political dichotomy and can be expressed in a variety of ways:

- Moral principles and the pursuit of the common good, opposed to 'the mundane principles... and the pursuit of one's own advantage'.

- In religious terms, the heavenly God opposed to the earthly god, Money or Mammon.

The quintessence of these antitheses is good versus evil. If ever there was a meaningful political dichotomy for all times, then here we have it.

---

[47] Marx quoted in Evola, p.329

The point Marx made was that everyone, Jew and gentile alike, had accepted the rule of Mammon. This had led to a universally accepted inversion of the norms of morality. In economics, the 'mundane principle' of pursuing 'one's own advantage' led to an acceptance of the view that private vices contribute to the common wealth. This would have been shocking to the medieval mind, even assuming it could understand it. The idea that benevolence is not really important, but that the pursuit of personal gain is, was the kind of thinking that the church councils of the high Middle Ages sought to expunge with the banning of usury.

> *It is not from the benevolence of the butcher, the brewer, or the baker, that we expect our dinner, but from their regard to their own interest. We address ourselves, not to their humanity but to their self-love, and never talk to them of our own necessities but of their advantages.* (Adam Smith, *The Wealth of Nations*.)

However acceptable to the modern world, Smith's statement would have been heresy to all levels of society in the Middle Ages, where the divine principle held sway.

If the political and economic orders are principally about 'egoism and selfish need', then science cannot be about speculating on the vertical order, the cosmic order, the harmonious chain of being. It is driven instead to analyse things so that we can better advance what we desire; it is about learning to exploit nature in such a way that the needs of the individual are satisfied. It was noted above that a money-based rule of quantity ensured that man's experience of space became just as desacralised as time, being equally indifferent to its contents. Science came to reflect this development by divorcing phenomena from their contexts. Science would from now on approach the world from a distance, with each phenomenon examined in isolation as a problem to be solved.

This single point of view of the absolute subject, who beholds objects that have been abstracted out of the real world, unworlded into an abstract space conditioned by mathematics, would have a revolutionising impact upon art, where 'egoism and selfish need' would find expression in the desacralised and homogeneous space that allowed for the development of depth-perspective. All images were subordinated to the point of view of a single subject who therefore determined all the properties of the phenomena within the frame. This was not an objective view of phenomena, it was highly subjective and representative of the position taken by western philosophy generally, i.e. the subject will dictate to phenomena how they will be. This distanced experience of the world was the polar-opposite to the total engagement and immersion of traditional man in hyper-realism.

In what Marx expressed as the Judaisation of civil society, all ties of familiarity would be slowly severed, leaving egoism and selfish need in the place of familial ties. In this world of 'atomistic individuals who are inimically opposed to one another', individual rights became the central concern of political philosophy, whether they eventually found expression on the political left or right. One side might argue that the coercive state is going to protect those individual rights, the other might say that a limited state is going to allow those individual rights to flourish. However, it is essentially no longer the general good, but the individual's pursuit of the good life that counts.

13 Disorder lived as order

Whilst engagement in economic activity in the Middle Ages had been justified to the extent of sustenance, the idea of founding a whole social philosophy upon economic motives would have been considered as base and brutish as we might think a system of human organisation based upon sexual instincts, only more so. Lives given over to personal economic gain (the sin of avarice or greed to the medieval mind), breeched the social ethics of attaining perfection within the social organism's multiplicity of relationships.

The traffickers of money, who eventually subverted the long-standing religious prohibition of usury, overcame the ethical objections to their 'mundane principles of... practical necessity and the pursuit of one's own advantage' by carving out an amoral zone, an apparently neutral sphere of commercial activity. What would once have been the very embodiment of sin, the notion that personal vices might have positive ends, emerged as civil society, complete with its own supporting covenantal 'theology' and philosophy of free will. Eventually thinkers such as Smith, Locke, Hobbes and Paine would codify the merging of Christianity once more into Judaism that Marx observed, as the secular political and economic creed of liberalism, or Whiggism as it was expressed in its early stages.

There was an ideological continuum, starting with the money traffickers running through to modernity, which was manifested in the apparition of freedom in politics, relegation of religion to a private pursuit, reduction of art to the artist's perspective and isolation of phenomena in the false objectivity of science. These attributes of modernity grew out of, and remain, founded upon money and the worship of Mammon. They are some of the defining characteristics of the money-based society.

The cultural and ethical divide between medieval Christendom and its subverters at the outset, lingers on in modernity as a grave suspicion of tradition. If what it means to be human and to be free is the unfolding of the individual's will and self-determination, then tradition would put an end to this. Tradition offers not radical freedom, but submission to a higher principle. So tradition tends to be viewed with hostility in modernity, by both the political left and right.

Liberalism's worship of the god of this world is the reenactment of the Fall feared by Luther. It is disorder lived as order, with the natural order now considered as repressive on many levels. Any meaningful opposition to modernity's inversion of this order demands therefore a restoration of the good versus evil antithesis as the central political dichotomy, replacing the false dichotomy of left and right that serves to uphold what in Marx's terms might be described as Judeo-liberalism, the extreme form of which is Marxism.

The corollary of this, however, is that there can be no reversion to tradition without a universally accepted belief in higher principles. The unity in multiplicity of tradition requires a hierarchy in the social organism that is accepted as an extension of the cosmic harmony. For the individual to renounce the absoluteness of his individual rights and consent to their relativity, without feeling that this renunciation is a resignation and a compromise, the radical traditionalists will have to offer a social structure based on something other than constraint.

To support the cause of good against evil means fighting for the dethronement of money, the subversion of the god of this world's rule by those who would submit as creatures to the Creator, as relative to the Absolute. By such an act of submission, all natures would gain access to a formal and qualitative equality, not horizontally amongst themselves, but vertically with regard to God.

The good versus evil dichotomy would be between the followers of a creator God on one side and the adherents of Mammon on the other, between religion and secularism, between traditionalism and liberalism. For there could be no reversion to tradition without a belief system. An absence of belief means no submission. An absence of submission means no restoration of hierarchy, and without a hierarchy the restoration of order is impossible.[48] Not surprisingly, it is in the interests of liberalism to promote atheism.

Perversely, today it is Mammonism that has the supporting 'belief' system - Calvinistic and covenantal. Disorder has taken upon itself the trappings of order to the point where the individual confronting traditionalism might say - 'I'm defending liberty and Christianity'. 'What is more, I'm defending liberty as a "tradition" of my country.' Thus anti-tradition takes on the trappings of religion and freedom for which people will die. It is a cruel and heartless deception, which means that, in the name of freedom, individuals are led to fight for their own enslavement; and as Julius Evola remarked, it is the worst form of enslavement.

---

[48] Frithjof Schuon wrote of Luther's basis for hierarchy in faith.

Just as the early Churches conceive a hierarchy that places monks and priests above the laity and the worldly, so also Luther—who had nothing of the revolutionary or even of the democrat in him—conceives a hierarchy that places those who truly live by faith above those who have not yet reached this point or are simply incapable of it. He intended to appeal to those who "willingly do what they know and are capable of acting with firm faith in the beneficence and favor of God" and "whom others ought to emulate"; but not to those who "make ill use of this freedom and rashly trust in it, so that they must be driven with laws, teachings, and warnings", and other formulations of this kind. (F. Schoun, 'The Question of Evangelism', taken from the collection of essays entitled *Ye Shall Know the Truth: Christianity and the Perennial Philosophy*, World Wisdom Books, Bloomington, 2005, p.28-9)

Since the modern view of life in its materialism has taken away from the single individual any possibility of bestowing on his destiny a transfiguring element and seeing in it a sign and a symbol, contemporary "slavery" should be reckoned as one of the gloomiest and most desperate kinds of all times.[49]

And what are these enslaved individuals most fearful of? The answer is tradition which, nominally, they are supposed to be defending. They are in reality defending the new paiduma that Luther feared: the Christian society turned Judaic recognised by Marx, the apparition of freedom experienced by atomised individuals in their increasingly commodified and clone-like status. They are defending a lie, whilst the state expunges diversity in the quest for equality of exchange and sale, quite apart from any social philosophy that might be guiding it. They are defending evil.

Failure to see the central antithesis running through history is a failure to understand history. It is to be deceived by liberalism's propagandistic history of 'progress' that is peddled shamelessly through the schooling system, media and Hollywood. Opposition to liberalism will demand the unveiling of truth, nothing short of a revision of history that places the central antithesis at its core.

---

[49] Evola, p.109

14 The Pilgrimage of Grace

Christian charity came face-to-face with Mammon and 'the mundane principles of Judaism', during the Pilgrimage of Grace in England, 1536, a popular rising and protest against Henry VIII's break with the Roman Catholic Church, the suppression of the monasteries, and the economic policies of the King's chief minister, Thomas Cromwell. This confrontation reflected the central antithesis of world history as it emerged in the post-Reformation world. The proponents of the vertical order made a stand against the horizontalism of disorder. Religion confronted secularism. Order stood against disorder. Traditionalism clashed with modernity and the future liberalism. The sacred and the profane collided.

The link between the sins of mankind and the wounds of Jesus was familiar in sixteenth century England.[50]

> *It was for this reason that the cult of the Five Wounds in England repeatedly expressed itself as acts of charity as well as Masses and prayers, and especially by acts of charity in multiples of fives,*

---

[50] M. W. Bloomfield, *The Seven Deadly Sins,* State College Press, Michegan, 1952, pp. 167-8, 189, 203, 205, 224.

*bestowed on Fridays and above all on Good Friday.
By such actual and symbolic charity one could turn
the wounds of judgement into the Wounds of
Mercy, forestalling the condemnation threatened in
Matthew 25 by attending, while there was still
time, to Christ's wounded members, the poor.*

Such charity towards the poor was linked intimately
with the health of the body of Christ, the church and,
therefore, the social organism as a whole. A banner bearing
the Holy wounds of Jesus Christ, was carried at the head
of the Pilgrimage of Grace.

*Into what appears to be a simple effective devotion
to the Passion, there was compressed the essence of
the practical soteriology of late medieval religion. It
is hardly surprising, therefore, that the symbol of
the Five Wounds should have been chosen by the
Pilgrims of Grace as the emblem of their loyalty to
the whole medieval Catholic system.*[51]

The religious houses that offered charitable care for the
sick and poor were symbolically tending the wounds of
Christ. The attack on the monasteries that prompted the
Pilgrimage of Grace was therefore an assault on the holistic
belief system within which men led their lives. And to
what end? Nothing less than mercantilism and commercial
gain, the sin of avarice. The defences of Christendom had

---

[51] E. Duffy, *The Stripping of the Altars: Traditional Religion in England
c.1400 - 1580*, Yale University Press, 2005, p.248

been well and truly breached. With Jericho-like vehemence, the objectors were swept out of the linear path of progress. Robert Aske the leader of the Pilgrimage was one of 216 martyrs who were brutally hung, drawn and quartered or burned to death.

15 Charles I's defence to the end of the vertical hierarchy

Charles I's last words on the scaffold had the historical central antithesis between the sacred way and the profane at their heart.

Many could not hear what he said as he spoke quietly. However, he was leaving his words for posterity. Charles directed his last comments to Colonel Tomlinson and Bishop Juxon who reported his words after the execution.

> *...all the world knows that I never did begin a War with the two Houses of Parliament... for I do believe that ill instruments between them and me has been the chief cause of all this bloodshed.*

He was acutely aware that there were larger forces, 'ill instruments', driving the war, other than the obvious protagonists. What did these 'ill instruments' have to gain from the defeat of the King? The answer to that, quite clearly, is commercial gain.

> *I have forgiven all the world, and even those in particular that have been the chief causes of my*

death. Who they are, God knows, I do not desire to know, God forgive them... For the people; And truly I desire their Liberty and Freedom as much as any Body whomsoever. But I must tell you, That their Liberty and Freedom, consists in having of Government; those Laws, by which their Life and their goods may be most their own. It is not for having share in government that is nothing pertaining to them. A subject and a sovereign are clean different things, and therefore until they do that, I mean, that you do put the people in that liberty as I say, certainly they will never enjoy themselves.

Charles I's defence to the end of the vertical hierarchy, the outward and imperfect expression of a supreme spiritual reality, was inevitably always going to clash with the new creed of 'practical necessity and the pursuit of one's own advantage'.

Charles's own position was best exemplified by his enthusiastic support for William Laud's enthronement as Archbishop of Canterbury. A champion of the social organism as a reflection of the natural order, Laud set himself against factionalism and the pursuit of individual economic gain. Factionalism in the form of parties was a threat to the coherence of society and had to be suppressed, for Governments must 'entertain no private business', and 'parties are ever private ends'. In the spirit of the medieval Church Councils, Laud detested as sacrilegious the self-interest which led the individual to struggle for riches and advancement. 'There is no private end, but in something or other it will be led to run cross the public: and, if gain come in, though it be by "making shrines for Diana", it is no matter with them though Ephesus be in an uproar for it.'[52]

Laud was executed by parliamentary forces in the midst of the Civil War for those beliefs, and Charles I was eventually overcome by the opponents who sought in Calvinism the halo of ethical sanctification for their amoral economic ends.

Charles concluded his final speech.

> *Sirs, It was for this that now I Am come here. If I would have given way to an Arbitrary way, for to have all Laws changed according to the power of the Sword, I needed not to have come here; and therefore, I tell you, (and I pray God it be not laid to your charge) That I Am the Martyr of the People... I have a good cause and a gracious GOD on my side.*

He could have given way to the forces of Mammon, disorder, the party with the greater financial backing and firepower, but he chose to make a stand for the natural order on earth. He offered himself to posterity as a martyr in the cause of the sacred way against the profane.

---

[52] Quoted in Tawney, p.175

16 Whig plotters and the Dutch invasion

After the civil war, Oliver Cromwell permitted the Jews to enter England again, but did not reverse the Edict of Expulsion issued by King Edward I in 1290, which expelled all Jews forever from England and made the provision that any who remained, after November 1st 1290, were to be executed.

No other symbolic action could have sent a stronger signal that, with the King's defeat, all resistance to usury in Britain had come to an end. It confirmed the beginning of the reign of disorder under the empire of Usura,[53] with the emergent political and economic creed of Whiggism at its heart.

Concomitant with the Calvinism of the victorious puritans who supported Cromwell was the opening up of the amoral economic sphere where, as Marx observed, life could be led in the 'spirit' of Judaism by all. 'Practical

---

[53] I have employed Ezra Pound's collective noun describing the distended western economy with its lopsided foundation upon banking and the principle of 'interest'. See Pound's Canto XLV, 'With Usura'.

necessity and the pursuit of one's own advantage' would rule the day and all political action would be directed towards supporting that end. Hence the sequence of events, in quick succession, that would change the direction of world history and be the source of conflict, death and misery to the present day.

The monarchy was restored in 1660, though Charles II reigned very much in the shadow of the newly empowered parliament. He was harmless to all Whiggish economic ambitions and ruled as an Anglican, hiding his religious and political sympathies until his deathbed conversion to Roman Catholicism. However, the much more forthright brother who succeeded Charles as James II of England and James VII of Scotland posed a problem to the Whigs.

He had landed in England with Charles as a seasoned and successful military campaigner, having served in the armies of the French King, Louis XIV. Thus it was as a military man he returned, which is why Charles appointed him Lord High Admiral. He held the position for 13 years with much success in the Dutch wars, building up the fleet and developing the use of gunpowder and artillery.

A strong and military-minded king was risk enough to Whiggish commercial ambitions, but when it was discovered that he too had converted to Roman Catholicism, then his fate was sealed.

The Dutch had no love of James for more reasons than religion. Whilst he was head of the English navy during the Dutch wars in 1666, English warships had sailed into the city of West Terschelling in the Netherlands and, on the 19th and 20th August, sank a large merchant fleet of 140 ships. During the same action West Terschelling was burnt down and completely destroyed.

It is highly likely that the Dutch started the Great Fire of London only two weeks later in an effective act of retaliation. The colourful Pudding Lane accident found in subsequent Whig histories is simply an outrageous coincidence peddled as truth by the heirs to the collaborators with the Dutch. The future King James II distinguished himself bravely as the leader of firefighting operations during the Great Fire. 'The Duke of York hath won the hearts of the people with his continual and indefatigable pains day and night in helping to quench the Fire', wrote a witness in a letter on 8 September.[54]

Whig plotters would have no trouble persuading potential adventurers from the financial centre of Amsterdam of the prize at hand. Access to new markets and use of English military power for financial and commercial ends was in prospect. This induced the gathering of a huge Dutch invasion force behind the bogus claim to the throne

---

[54] Spelling modernised for clarity; quoted by A. Tinniswood, *By Permission of Heaven: The Story of the Great Fire of London,* Jonathan Cape London, 2003, p.80.

of William of Orange. The fleet that carried William to England contained 463 ships and 40,000 men. It was almost twice the size of the Armada sent by Philip of Spain one hundred years before.

Just 33 years after Cromwell signalled that England was open to usury, financial interests inside and outside the country had collaborated to depose the last living embodiment of divinely sanctioned power. William and Mary were figureheads. Money ruled. Only six years later, the Bank of England would be established.

17 The twin pillars of Usura

Within six years of deposing the rightful King of England, the Dutch financiers from Amsterdam who had backed the invasion of Britain, nominally under the leadership of William of Orange, together with their English Whig collaborators, sought to exact their return, with interest. They would fulfil their objective of taking control of the British economy, whilst installing themselves as its real governing force. This they did by establishing the Bank of England, the merits of which to its supporters were summed up in the oft-repeated sentence by its nominal founder, William Patterson: 'the Bank hath benefit of interest on all monies which it creates out of nothing'.[55]

The bank would be enforced as the only source from which government officials could borrow money, with the debt secured against public taxes. The country sold bonds to the bank in return for money it could not raise in taxes. The bonds were paid for by money produced from thin air. The government paid interest on the money it borrowed by borrowing more money in the same way.

---

[55] Quoted in C. Hollis, *Two Nations, A Financial Study of English History*, George Routledge and Sons, London, 1935, p. 36.

There was no way this debt could ever be paid back. The scam enslaved all who lived under its rule.

Enough has been written about the scourge of fractional reserve banking, as this legalised counterfeiting has been called, without going into detail here. Suffice it to say that, in times of economic upheaval, wealth is rarely destroyed and instead is only transferred. And it is those interests that control the money supply who benefit the most when money is scarce. When the majority of people are suffering through economic depression, you can be sure that these interests are continuing to get rich.

With the Dutch invasion of England and the founding of the Bank of England, the empire of Usura entered history. Its hallmarks were power through the seizure of the money supply and the build-up of military might. These are what enticed the backers and collaborators of the invasion. These would be the twin pillars of Usura from this point on. Of the first £1.2m raised as a loan with the Bank of England, half was spent on the building of warships. The omens were there right from the start.

18 The Usurocracy[56] and the mob

It all began with money, the trafficking of money and illegal money-lending by a minority of outsiders who were forced to hide within the very pores of the social organism. Usura was born of a long and bitter struggle between the usurer and the rest of mankind. That which was once held to be profane, permitted grudgingly to serve the people in only a limited way, had now usurped power.

There is no neutral position. To view Whig history as though it represented an enlightened rationality is to choose the path of Pharisaic self-righteousness. It is a choice that has had catastrophic consequences for millions upon millions of people since Usura was founded, and continues to do so with increasing ferociousness to this very day.

The founders of Usura renounced love, embracing instead power and gold in the manner of Wagner's Alberich the Nibelung. Sings Alberich addressing the old gods...

---

[56] Another favourite collective noun of Ezra Pound's, see for example, E. Pound, *Selected Prose,* Faber and Faber, London, 1973, pp.161, 309 and 342.

You who aloft in the soft zephyrs' breeze
live,
laugh and love,
all you gods I'll grip
in my golden grasp!
As I renounced love,
all living things
shall renounce it!
Allured by gold,
for gold alone shall you hunger.
On radiant peaks
you live,
lulled in bliss:
the black gnome
you despise, you eternal revellers!
Beware!
Beware!

With the seizure of power came the manipulation of the masses. By 1700, London was the largest city in the world with over 500,000 inhabitants. In the London mob, the new money interests ruling England, the Usurocracy, had a ready-made means of securing its grip on power, and it ensured that it could steer the mob in any direction it wanted with the introduction of nationalistic patriotism. After the Act of Union in 1715, the Union Jack became the symbol of this new Whiggism. Thomas Arne wrote the music to match the sentiment. In 1740, theatre audiences were singing along to his *Rule Britannia* and, by 1745, standing to *God Save the King*. The mob that had so recently been enslaved to the national debt was induced to sing, with the cruelest irony, that 'Britons never, never, never shall be slaves'. The timing of these instruments of psychological enslavement conditioned minds in readiness for the '45 rebellion, a lost cause from the start given its disorganisation, but buoyed along remarkably by popular sentiment for the restoration of the rightful king, particularly in the North, where the instruments of Usura's propaganda had not yet penetrated. Less than a hundred years later, the Usurocracy felt it safe enough to unleash democracy as its means of securing power against those who could see through its façade of governance to the rottenness of legalised counterfeiting corruption at its core. To this day, the Usurocracy relies on mob rule to maintain and extend its power. It fights wars to extend its grip over the money supply in the name of democracy.

19 The American Revolution: a serious rival to Usura established

Compared to Usura's next war, the '45 was a localised skirmish. Winston Churchill described the Seven Years War of 1756-1763 as the first real world war.[57] It was the first conflict in human history to be fought around the globe, certainly. However, and Churchill was no doubt conscious of this point, it was also defined as global by being Usura's first engagement in a war for the world - for the economic control of the world and the hearts, minds and souls of its inhabitants.

By the end of the war, Usura had secured the control over North America and India. The very next year, in 1764, Usura set about expanding the tax base to include the North American colonies, as a means of securing the ever-mounting debt. Since the creation of the Bank of England, the total debt stood at £140,000,000. The rest, as they say, is history, but certainly not Whig history.

There is enough material available with which to piece together the incredible story of Usura's rise and rise,

---

[57] H.V. Bowen, *War and British Society 1688-1815,* Cambridge University Press, Cambridge, 1988, p.7

without examining the phenomenon in too much detail here. It is important to note, however, the importance of Ezra Pound's pioneering work in this field, particularly on the subject of Usura's extension of control over the United States. He said, in one of his notorious radio speeches from Mussolini's Italy during the Second World War, that 'The present war dates at least from the founding of the Bank of England at the end of the 17th century'.[58] Such a statement was never likely to dissuade American GIs from landing on the Italian coast as he had hoped, but it did demonstrate an insight into the causes of Usura's wars that has provided a foundation for revisionist study ever since.

As soon as the attention turned to taxing the Americans, the British-based banking interests found the colonialists printing their own paper money, known as colonial scrip. The American colonies were a particularly attractive tax prospect, because of their prosperity.

The debt free issue of currency on such a scale in the colonies posed a threat to the interest charging power of the Usurocracy, which hurriedly pressed the British Parliament to pass the 1764 Currency Act. This action immediately suppressed the printing of money by the colonists, and forced them to pay taxes to Britain in silver

---

[58] From *Ezra Pound Speaking, Radio Speeches of World War II,* Edited by L. W. Doob, Greenwood Press, Westport, Connecticut and London, 1978, speech no. 70 (March 25, 1943) 'To Recapitulate'.

or gold. In this draconian measure lay the principle cause of Usura's next conflict, the American Revolutionary War of 1775–1783. It had nothing to do with the more picturesque matters, such as the Boston Tea Party of the Whig history books, which was just as much a diversion from the truth as the Pudding Lane origins of London's great fire.

Such was the centrality of the money issue to the cause of the American revolutionists that upon victory, the power allotted to Congress 'to coin money and regulate the value thereof' was included in the Constitution of the new nation. The bankers were excluded. A serious rival to Usura had been established.

20 Usura's endless wars

In 1790, Mayer Amschel Rothschild was alleged to have said, 'let me issue and control a nation's money and I care not who writes the laws'.[59] Certainly in keeping with this maxim, whoever said it, the Usurocracy decided that its interests would be best served by allowing America independence, whilst establishing a 'national bank' on US soil, which English bankers would then control. Thereafter, repeated attempts to establish a US equivalent to the Bank of England succeeded temporarily, only to be defeated by dogged opposition from founding father notables.

The renewal of the charter for the First Bank of the United States was vetoed by Congress in 1811 on the grounds that it was unconstitutional. Within five months of making this stand against a central bank, the young nation was plunged into another war with Usura. Britain attacked America and started the war of 1812. With conflict raging across land and sea for 32 months, the war achieved no territorial change between either side. However, Usura secured a victory of sorts as, by 1816, faced with economic

---

[59] First attributed to Rothschild by Gertrude M. Coogan in *Money Creators*, Sound Money Press, Chicago, 1935, very last sentence of Ch. 16

hardship from the war, Congress approved a second national bank.

Whilst Usura waged war upon America, Napoleon's struggle against the twin forces of money supply control and military might was drawing to a close. Everywhere Napoleon went at the head of his conquering armies, he found that Usura had already been there before him. The Bank of England made huge profits as Prussia, Austria and finally Russia all went heavily into debt trying to stop him.

Unwilling to subject himself to the control of bankers through their issue of credit, both as Consul and then as Emperor, Napoleon had stubbornly refused to borrow. Louis Bergeron argued that Napoleon was inspired 'by a rigid sense of the dignity of the state, since the public power should not depend on bankers and merchants'.[60] Napoleon steadily refused to create paper money; he even forbade the general circulation of banknotes.

Instead of resorting to the banks, Napoleon sold territory west of the Mississippi to the United States for $15 million in gold; a deal known as the Louisiana Purchase.[61]

---

[60] L. Bergeron, *France Under Napoleon*, trans. Robert R. Palmer, Princeton University Press, 1981, p.41

[61] C. A. Cerami, *Jefferson's Great Gamble: The Remarkable Story of Jefferson, Napoleon and the Men behind the Louisiana Purchase*, Sourcebooks, Illinois, 2003, p.204

He added to his war chest through the 'confiscations of feudal and crown properties, real and personal, in defeated countries; the spoils taken directly from the enemy; the war indemnities in money and in kind, "justified" by the right of conquest or provided for in imposed treaties of peace.' This source of funds 'not only covered the needs of the armies but produced considerable surpluses, to which Napoleon alluded when he asserted, "I brought over two thousand million in specie into France," or when he claimed at St Helena, that he had "left 400 million in the cellars of the Tuilleries"'.[62]

An attack from Spain in the south financed by Rothschild and other serious defeats eventually overwhelmed France, forcing Napoleon into exile on Elba. Even before the later Battle of Waterloo, Usura's victory was complete. Napoleon was forced to raise money from the banker Gabriel-Julien Ouvrard and others to make his last 100 days bid for glory. Whatever the outcome of Waterloo, control over the money supply would remain in the Usurocracy's hands, and it would 'care not who writes the laws'. True to the maxim, after Napoleon's final defeat at Waterloo, the bankers finally took control of the French finances.

In 1815, the Allies demanded an indemnity of 700,000,000 francs from the defeated French. How on earth would the French come up with that kind of money? Ouvard's solution was to float a bond issue in London. He obtained

[62] Bergeron, p.40

permission from the Duke of Wellington, the general of the Allied occupying army in France, while merchant bankers Barings and Hope & Co syndicated the loan, with the debt secured against the public taxes of France.[63] Now, like the British, French taxpayers were paying the bankers back, with interest, for a loan on money that had been created 'out of nothing'. France was in the clutches of the expanding Usura.

With Usura's triumvirate empire of Britain, France and America seemingly secure on both sides of the Atlantic, the Americans rebelled again. In 1832, President Andrew Jackson personally vetoed another move to renew the charter of the Second Bank of the US, becoming the only president whose administration totally abolished the national debt. When asked what was the greatest achievement of his career, Jackson replied, 'I killed the bank'.

Only three years after the veto, there was a failed assassination attempt on Jackson's life. Usura was held at bay, but would not let go. A growing world power with massive resources and scope for taxation would not be tolerated long outside of the central banking system. A divide and conquer opportunity to redress matters came in 1861 with the American Civil War, thus qualifying it as yet another of Usura's endless wars.

---

[63] D. Landes, *Dynasties: Fortune and Misfortune in the World's Great Family Businesses*, Penguin, New York, 2007, Part 1, section 1

21 History NOT according to Spielberg

There is an alternative history of the American Civil War. An opinion attributed to Otto Von Bismark epitomised the counter-view to the official history of Lincoln's abolitionist war, and certainly supports the thesis that the unfolding of events had more to do with Usura's expansionist aspirations than slavery.

With the clarity of hindsight, the Chancellor of the rising German state, a country still beyond Usura'a borders, was reported to have made the following statement in 1876.

> *The division of the United States into federations of equal force was decided long before the Civil War by the high financial powers of Europe, these bankers were afraid that the United States if they remained as one block and as one nation, would attain economic and financial independence which would upset their financial domination over the world.*

Of the Usurocracy, Bismark was reported as saying:

...they foresaw the tremendous booty if they could substitute two feeble democracies, indebted to the financiers, to the vigorous Republic, confident and self-providing. Therefore they started their emissaries in order to exploit the question of slavery and thus dig an abyss between the two parts of the Republic.[64]

Lincoln stood no chance of obtaining war loans at realistic interest rates from the money lenders who wanted the Union to fail. The solution to the problem was the 'greenback', effectively the resurrection of colonial scrip. Upon taking action to print $450 million worth of greenbacks, Lincoln made this statement of defiance to the forces of Usura intent upon undermining the Union's cause.

The government should create, issue and circulate all the currency and credit needed to satisfy the spending power of the government and the buying power of consumers... The privilege of creating and issuing money is not only the supreme prerogative of Government, but it is the Government's greatest creative opportunity. By the adoption of these principles, the long-felt want for a uniform medium will be satisfied. The taxpayers will be saved immense sums of interest, discounts and exchanges.

---

[64] Quoted in Count Cherep-Spiridovich, *The Secret World Government or 'The Hidden Hand'*, The Anti-Bolshevist Publishing Association, New York, 1926, p. 180.

The financing of all public enterprises, the maintenance of stable government and ordered progress, and the conduct of the Treasury will become matters of practical administration. The people can and will be furnished with a currency as safe as their own government. Money will cease to be the master and become the servant of humanity. Democracy will rise superior to the money power.[65]

It was a defiance for which he would pay dearly shortly after the war ended.

Tsar Alexander II of Russia, who continued to fend off the forces of Usura, blocking their attempts to achieve a foothold in his own country, recognised a potential ally in the Americans if only they could successfully resist the Usurocracy's efforts to split their country. As early as 1861, Russia alerted the Lincoln government to the machinations of Napoleon III, who was already scheming to promote a joint British, French and Russian intervention in favour of the Confederacy.[66] Russia would have no part in this and intervention was avoided because of British and French fears of what Russia might do if they

---

[65] Quoted in *Senate Document 23, National Economy and the Banking System of the United States: An exposition of the principles of modern monetary science in their relation to the national economy and the banking system of the United States,* by R. L. Owen, United States, Government Printing Office, Washington, 1939, p.91

[66] J. W. Foster, *A Century of American Diplomacy 1776-1876,* Houghton Mifflin, Boston, 1900, p. 372

continued to launch bellicose gestures against the Union. On October 29, 1862 there occurred in St. Petersburg an extremely cordial meeting of Russian Foreign Minister Gortchakov with US Chargé d'Affaires Bayard Taylor, which was marked by a formal Russian pledge never to move against the US, and to oppose any attempt by other powers to do so.[67] The Tsar declared that if France or Britain gave help to the South, Russia would consider this an act of war. In making this declaration of support for Lincoln's opposition to Usura, he declared himself an enemy of the bankers too.

In 1863, with victory in sight, Lincoln was desperate for more funds to complete his final push. Having ensured that Lincoln would get no further support from Congress for the issue of more greenbacks, the representatives of the Usurocracy proposed the passing of the National Bank Act. The act went through. From this point on the entire US money supply would be created out of debt by bankers buying US government bonds and issuing them from reserves for bank notes.

Given Lincoln's enthusiasm for the state issue of 'all the currency and credit needed to satisfy the spending power of the government and the buying power of consumers', it is certain that he would have reversed the National Bank Act after gaining renewed public support in his re-

---

[67] US Department of State, *Papers relating to the foreign relations of the United States, Bayard Taylor to Secretary Seward*, October 29,1862, Government Printing Office, Washington DC, 1864, Part II, p. 764

election victory. That is, had he not been assassinated only forty one days after being re-elected. The National Bank Act was safe but, if Bismark was right, it had taken a highly mechanised and vicious war, with the resultant death of millions, to make it so.

22 All the backbone of Jefferson's thought and of Van Buren's forgotten!

Only sixteen years after Abraham Lincoln's assassination, President James Garfield met the same bloody fate, even though he did not support the greenback and conceded that paper should be backed by silver and gold. He was resolute in affirming however that Congress should be master of the money supply. In his inaugural address he insisted that it was 'the chief duty of the National Government in connection with the currency of the country is to coin money and declare its value'.[68]

Tzar Alexander II was assassinated in the same year, following several attempts on his life since 1866, shortly after Lincoln's death. However, Russia remained beyond the clutches of Usura, and the murdered Tzar was succeeded by his son, Alexander III.

When the time came to formalise and monopolise an American economy based on government debt, the outcome was almost anti-climactic. On 23rd December 1913

---

[68] J. A. Garfield, *Inaugural Address,* Friday, March 4, 1881, quoted on http://www.bartleby.com/124/pres36.html Citation dated 29.11.13

the House of Representatives passed the Federal Reserve Act, but it was still having difficulty in its passage through the Senate. Most members of Congress had gone home for the holidays, but the Senate had not adjourned and was technically still in session. There were only three members still present. On a unanimous consent voice vote, the 1913 Federal Reserve Act was passed. No objection was made, because there was no one there to object.

Anti-climactic this may have been, but the impact of America's formal assumption into Usura's empire of central banking was to be devastating and world-changing in the century of world wars ahead. The First World War started almost immediately after the US was securely within the central banking system.

Ezra Pound made the insightful observation that 'A nation that will not get itself into debt drives the usurers to fury'. And it would indeed appear that the allied powers of Usura (Britain, France and USA) have waged war against countries that have resisted the debt-based financing of central banks, more recently resource-rich Iraq, Libya and Syria.

World War One started between Austria-Hungary and Serbia, but quickly turned into a war between Usura and Germany. Although pre-war Germany had a private central bank, it was heavily restricted and inflation kept to reasonable levels. Under firm government control, invest-ment was guaranteed to internal economic development, and, in the late nineteenth and early twentieth centuries, Germany's economic growth was outstripping those of Britain and France. Put simply, Germany was a threat to Usura's dominance.

This was especially so once Germany had agreed the construction of a Baghdad to Berlin railway with the Ottoman Empire, a strategic supply line which threatened Usura's monopoly access to oil in the Middle East. The threat from this railway, which was in fact planned to extend to Basra, was all the more critical because of Britain's decision to switch its vast navy from coal to oil as a source of fuel.

The German railway would provide direct access to Middle Eastern oil and bypass the British and French controlled Suez Canal. Germany was moving ahead and clearly threatened Britain's global hegemony. It is perhaps not surprising after all that the first deployment of British troops, once war was declared, went to Basra, not the fields of Flanders.

Widening the sphere of central banking and the protection of monopoly oil investments are much more credible candidates for the causes of war with Germany than the incident at Sarajevo, the stuff of Whig history. America's late entry to the war was for no other reason than to kill off the external threat to Usura's expansionist ambitions. Committing aid to its two former colonial masters would otherwise have been perverse, as indeed it appeared to many Americans at the time. The infamous Balfour Agreement may have had a role in persuading the Jewish banking interests behind the U.S. government to lobby for support for Britain, in return for a Zionist homeland on Palestinian land. However, this strong possibility is surplus to the geopolitical reasons already stated.

Entering the War, there were many empires. Leaving it, there was only one, Usura, the combined forces of Britain, France and the U.S.

In the aftermath of war, Germany's private central bank, to which Germany had gone deeply into debt to pay the reparations exacted by the Treaty of Versailles, broke free of government control and massive inflation followed (mostly triggered by currency speculators), permanently trapping the German people in endless debt. When the Weimar Republic collapsed economically, it opened the door for economic renewal.

Obtaining dispassionate historical analyses of the German economy as it stood before the Second World War is impossible. The control over the interpretation of the events of that era is central to the current political settlement and will not be relinquished in a hurry. What everyone does agree upon is the fact that from 1933 Germany experienced an economic growth spurt. It appears that this coincided with an abandonment of a gold-backed currency, with the result that barter, the direct exchange of goods, became possible in international trade. An example of this is Germany's exchange of locomotives for Argentinean beef, which did not require international trading credits or a reserve currency.

The underpinning principle of economic policy was one promulgated by Gottfried Feder, which was that labour creates value, not gold. In an attempt to apply this principle, the German government introduced bills of credit, known as mefo-wechsel, to the value of 5.5 billion Reichsmarks. This was added to the 4.5 billion Reichsmarks allowed under the Treaty of Versailles until 1933. German heavy industry, including Siemens, Krupp, and AEG, undertook to cover these bills of exchange in such a way that their fixed industrial assets provided security for the newly created money. This enabled the creation of up to 10 billion Reichsmarks, the minimum amount required to boost the economy in a work-for-work exchange system. After this medium of exchange was established, contracts for residential construction, autobahn highways and the modernisation of agriculture began immediately.

The 'problem' with this state-issued value-based currency was that it placed Germany outside of the global economic system. Once again, Germany was emerging as a threat to the dominance of Usura.

It was in the context of similar economic developments that Ezra Pound drew a comparison between Italy and the America of the Jefferson years. The United States in its post-revolutionary era had once stood against the expanding might of Usura. Pound in his wartime radio broadcasts reminded the American public of that lost history. He had already written of the 'laziness of whole generations!, All the backbone of Jefferson's thought and of Van Buren's forgotten! Benefits of the latter, lost in civil war and post-civil war finance!'[69]

As early as 1933, a global economic boycott was organised against Germany,[70] a regime that was attempting to operate outside the purview of the central bankers. In 1939, as Germany's booming full-employment economy began to flex its muscles against the restrictions of the Versailles Treaty, Usura felt compelled to declare war.

'The aim of finance is always to gain by other's labour', wrote Ezra Pound. Ultimately, this has to be imposed by force. War, in the modern context, is the compulsion of one to work for another in the aggregate, writ large. The renunciation of love for power and gold was no neutral choice. The triumph of a credo once held by a minority, forced by circumstances to live on the margins of society, was neither progress nor rationality, as the current superstructure of ideas in philosophy, science and art might have us believe. This was enslavement, enforced militarily. No wonder the vertically-orientated societies of Russia and Japan were horizontalised by Usura - one

---

[69] E. Pound, *ABC of Economics,* Faber and Faber, London, 1933, p.63

[70] B. Lang, *Philosophical Witnessing: The Holocaust as Presence,* Brandeis University Press, 2009, p.132

by financial support from bankers for a small and violent coterie intent on revolution, the other, literally, by atomic bombs.

The last great target for assimilation by Usura is Islam and the last vestige of theocratic rule in Iran. It is the denouement to this confrontation that lies at the heart of the present global crisis, which had its origins in 1694 with the founding of the Bank of England.

23 Edmund Burke and regime legitimisation

The most earth-shattering revolution the world has ever seen, ultimately with the most violent of consequences for countless millions of its victims to this very day, was described by its propagandists as a victory for moderation.

Whig historians of the so-called Glorious Revolution in Britain have always worked on the basis that if you are going to tell a lie, you might as well make it a big one. Edmund Burke (1729-1797), that hero of Anglo-Saxon conservatism, in reality liberalism, set the tone for the historical analysis that continues largely unchanged to this day. He proclaimed that 'The Revolution was made to preserve our ancient indisputable laws and liberties, and that ancient constitution of government which is our only security for law and liberty'. The English, Burke argued, were not creating a new regime, merely restoring the old one that had been distorted by the Catholic James II. 'The very idea of the fabrication of a new government is enough to fill us with disgust and horror,' Burke concluded.

Burke wrote these words in his *Reflections on the Revolution in France* in 1790, just over one hundred years after the usurpation of the British throne by Dutch financiers and their Whig aristocratic collaborators. He was either oblivious to the significance of this coup d'état, or a propagandist in its service. His work was contrived to give an air of historical legitimacy and continuity to the new banker regime in Britain after 1688, even to the point of fooling avowed French counter-revolutionist and Burke-admirer, Joseph de Maistre (1753-1821).

Legitimacy was vital to the occupiers of the new and remodelled country estates that were springing up all over eighteenth century Britain. For these beneficiaries of the coup, the revolution must have seemed truly glorious. Burke's work of regime legitimisation was continued after him by Thomas Babington Macaulay, who wrote of the 1688 coup that this 'was a revolution strictly defensive, and had prescription and legitimacy on its side'. Macaulay's great nephew George Macaulay Trevelyan was equally propagandistic in his disinformation. Trevelyan opined that 'the spirit of this strange Revolution was the opposite of revolutionary'.

Burke indeed was a supporter of the American revolutionists, but this was strictly from a Whig perspective and therefore wholly consistent with his enthusiasm for the so-called Glorious Revolution. His famous 1775 parliamentary speech was more about the commercial benefits of a reconciliation with the colonists than their ultimate liberty. Recognising this, the traditionalist Samuel Johnson penned a parody of Burke's speech, in which the devil says of the Americans:

> *Be not dispirited then at the contemplation of their present happy state: I promise you that anarchy, poverty, and death shall, by my care, be earned even across the spacious Atlantic, and settle in America itself, the sure consequences of our beloved whiggism.*[71]

The erection of the statue of Burke in Washington in 1922 coincided not only with the shifting centre of Usura's power, but also marked the ultimate rejection by the U.S. of its former history of resistance to usurious banking power - the sure consequence of 'our beloved whiggism'.

---

[71] *Johnsoniana: Anecdotes of the Late Samuel Johnson LL.D, Mrs Piozzi, Richard Cumberland, Bishop Percy and others together with the diary of Dr Campbell and Extracts from that of Madame D'Aeblay newly collected and edited by Eobina Napier*, London, George Bell and Sons, York Street, Covent Garden, and New York, 1892, pp.20-1

24 Emile Keller's counter-revolutionism

Edmund Burke's contrasting of the so-called Glorious Revolution with the French Revolution was but a superficial window-dressing of history. He and the Whig historians who followed him, simply rendered events acceptable to the Whig collaborators who, on their newly updated and porticoed country estates, were welcoming the money-lenders into their social circles and families. To say the Glorious Revolution was a peaceful handover of power neglected the extended and bloody struggle that led up to it, namely the English Civil War and Dutch Wars. The outcome of the revolutions in Britain and France was certainly the same: financial freedom for the beneficiaries of uncontrolled usury and the fractional reserve lending of central banking.

In contrast to the lickspittle Whig histories, the French counter-revolutionists described the aftermath of financial freedom as anything but glorious. Emile Keller's account, written in 1865, remains just as relevant to this day. 'The poor and the state itself', wrote Keller, 'found themselves at the mercy of capital, which had complete licence to sell, to buy, to speculate, to charge fees, to retain funds, or to lend at high rates'. Keller elaborated the implications of financial freedom, which later became the credo of liberalism, the dominant ideology of Usura.

The newly emancipated wealth was quick to refuse those free services that hitherto had been regarded as an honour to render to the country. In confiscating the goods of the clergy, great care was taken to leave to the state's expense, and thus to the nation's the provision of education, charity, and worship that the church had originally provided.

With the one hand they had pushed away the work of pure devotion, with the other they had grabbed the best ranks, offices, and functions that the nation dispensed.

The country now has the obligation to pay a triple army of soldiers, employees, and creditors, an army that grows each day and whose general staff is drawn from a small circle of favoured families. Thus, in place of a great reservoir of natural riches on which each could draw, we have a public debt of ten billions... Thanks to this predominance of material interests, the aristocracy of devotion, virtue, talent, military honour, judicial integrity, and municipal patriotism is everywhere eclipsed by the aristocracy - or better, by the feudal barons - of finance, the basest and most self-serving of all.

Today, we have financial liberty, an absolutism of capital freed from all laws - human and divine - and dealing mortal wounds to the social liberty it claims to have founded.

For the man with nothing, equality under the law, social liberty, political liberty, and religious liberty are mere decoys.

Thence comes - and think deeply on it - the inevitable menace of war and social revolution, the mere spectre of which froze the bourgeoisie in terror in 1848. At the end of these violent struggles came the no less lamentable necessity of a new centralisation, a new absolutism of the state on the economic terrain.

The country will resemble a giant railroad company, incapable of managing its own fortune, hardly knowing those who are chosen to represent her, and whose hearts, minds, arms, and fortunes will be at the mercy of several braided helmets, at once all-powerful and irresponsible.[72]

Now, instead of the country as one giant railroad company, we might think of the world approaching the globalised state of one giant enterprise. Financial liberty - or liberalism - remains at its heart.

---

[72] É. Keller in *Critics of the Enlightenment: Readings in the French Counter-Revolutionary Tradition,* Edited and translated by Christopher Olaf Blum, ISI Books, Wilmington, 2003, pp. 277-294

Liberalism, which started with money and was founded on the 'mundane principles of pursuing one's own advantage', the universal outlook described as Judaic by Marx, became the dominant ideology of Usura. The 'education' of the masses ensured liberalism's deep-rootedness, with science and the aptly named humanities - politics, economics, the arts and philosophy - all serving to reinforce its dominance. The controlled mass-media ensured the belief was nurtured throughout life, through entertainment as well as misinformation. Even the remnants of religion in the West were now to have liberalism as their guiding 'ethic'.

25 The ignorance upon which finance thrives

It did not take long after the French Revolution for Louis-Gabriel-Ambrose de Bonald to recognise that a devotion to science and the study of material things was complementary to the thriving of commerce. It led, however, to a decline of the mind and reason.

> *I even believe that a people exclusively devoted to the study of material things - which improve no other faculty than the student's memory - will eventually become inferior to other peoples with respect to the mind, reason, and other social qualities... Their mercantile commerce will be able to flourish, but their social commerce will be little agreeable.*[73]

Bonald recognised the ignorance upon which finance thrived, an ignorance which Ezra Pound later described as antithetic to discrimination by the senses.

---

[73] Louis-Gabriel-Ambrose de Bonald in *Critics of the Enlightenment*, p. 60.

Discrimination by the senses is dangerous to avarice. It is dangerous because any perception or any high development of the perceptive facilities may lead to knowledge. The money-changer only thrives on ignorance.

He thrives on all sorts of insensitivity and non-perception. An instant sense of proportion imperils financiers.

You can, by contrast, always get financial backing for debauchery. Any form of 'entertainment' that debases perception, anything that profanes the mysteries or tends to obscure discrimination, goes hand in hand with drives towards money profit.[74]

In such conditions of carefully nurtured mass ignorance, the Usurocracy can depend on democracy as a safe and efficient instrument of dominance and control. The separate political parties of Usura represent but the separate wings and tendencies of liberalism in what is, in effect, one party rule. Challenges to the money-based power which, given the nature of liberal society, will only ever be from a small minority of enlightened individuals are thus banished to the margins.

Liberalism and all that goes with it is the ideology that Usura seeks to impose upon the world. Britain, France and the USA are still in the business of exporting the

---

[74] Pound, *Guide to Kulchur*, p.281

French Revolution, where necessary through war. And in the name of what are these wars fought? Liberty and democracy. And what follows? A thing known commonly as 'the winning of hearts and minds', through education, entertainment and misinformation - in short, indoctrination. And what is the result? The ignorance upon which finance thrives.

26 A template for social organisation

It is vitally important that we never lose sight of the connection between contemporary liberalism and its inglorious past. It was a regressive development, rather than the result of progress as understood by the progressivist ideologues of modernity. Liberalism's rise was triggered by usury and the trafficking of money, which led western society to take a wrong turn in the sixteenth century. Manipulating the masses through the media and indoctrination (compulsory, curriculum-controlled education), the perpetrators of liberalism are by default the defenders of the money power and worshippers of Mammon.

In short, liberalism does not have a case to make - other than to the supporters and perpetuators of evil. Having established that much, traditionalism can present its own case, having torn the sanctimonious mask from the defenders of disorder as order.

Disorder can only be lived as order for so long. Despair may be denied, but a life of inauthenticity will only store up its message of terror for the denier until the point at which no more can be done. If at no other time, the dread realisation of a lifetime of inauthenticity and despair will hit the denier at the threshold of death. This indeed was Heidegger's point in describing the moment when the individual is exposed to what he really is, when the world has nothing more to say to him and he has no choice but to confront himself.

The implication of this is that, to live authentically, we must somehow live our lives as if before death, before the Creator; because as the created we cannot lie to the Creator. The eradication of despair, as Kierkegaard argued, 'occurs when the self, in relating to itself and in wanting to be itself, is grounded nakedly in the power that established it'.[75]

This is the polar opposite of Nietzsche's 'will to power', that human-centric culmination of western philosophy by which we seek to dominate being rather than understand it. If the fulfilment of Nietzsche's 'will to power' results in a life lead at the height of inauthenticity, then its opposite, authenticity, must come from the relinquishing of power. Rather than imposing the self upon being, the authentic self must, as Heidegger explained, become the 'shepherd of being'.[76]

---

[75] *Kierkegaard*, p.136

[76] M. Heidegger, *Letter on Humanism*, in *Basic Writings*, ed. David Farrell Krell, Routledge, Kegan and Paul, Abingdon, 1978, p. 245

The Shepherd, died, naked, upon the cross as the paschal lamb. If, in Jean Borella's words, 'we needed to wait for the Incarnation of that One who is Truth, infinite Wisdom, Sun of Justice, Hypostatic Hierarchy, the Divine Word, for the injustice of sin to be fully and totally revealed', we also needed the sacrifice of that One who is Truth to understand how order might be restored. This was authentic sacrifice, the ultimate relinquishment of power, an example to all of how those who live as if before death disempower themselves before hierarchy.

The spiritual and social implications of this example are inseparable, and offer traditionalists a template for social organisation in the future, as they once did in the past. There would, for example, be no amoral economic realm, in which the 'mundane principles of Judiasm', as Marx described them, or the self-love and self-interest of Smith's economic actors, could burgeon again into dominance. An authentic life would be one of obligation and, through submission to the vertical order in a social organism, all roles would be service. As one body, man would reverence being, shepherd being and thereby confront the truth. Life would be one of rite, rather than flight. Our wills would indeed 'become one single will'[77] in this respect, in a hierarchy of service to the truth, to the Creator.

No role would escape submission and, in full knowledge of this, the burden of the sacred act of leadership would

[77] *Paradiso* Canto III l. 81

also be accepted as sacrifice. Recognised as such, and ameliorated by the reverence of others, leadership must also be a sacred act of gnosis, or it will be evil. In other words, the motive of leadership would be sacrifice, rather than the power that defines leadership in the modern world.

If defiance, power, or evil, were not loose in the world, a warrior prince would not be needed. As it is, the way to the truth must be fought for. The pilgrimage routes need protecting, be they the pathways of the mind or those of the earthly road. War is just if it resists evil, power and inauthenticity, which means war against the god of this world and his minions, holy war.

A traditionalist society would be one in which this world's values are inverted, for it is the meek who will inherit the earth. This is the truth; the natural, cosmic and Creator's order. Willing submission to the hierarchy would not be a compromise. It would be the sacred act through which freedom, authenticity and reality are recovered from the kali yuga pit of liberalism.

27 The economy will exist to serve the people

In opposition to the eradication of despair on a global scale stand the Usura regimes run by the princes of this world, the bankers and money lenders, with their twin-pillars of power: control over the money supply and military might.

These perpetuators of despair have led us into the desacralised realm, known as liberal society, 'legitimised' by sham democracies in which the masses are manipulated through indoctrination and the media. The result is a fallen world in which disorder is lived as order. The guiding organisational principles are those of corporate HR, imposing equality and killing diversity. Its false worldview is horizontal in orientation.

The world is run on the 'mundane principles' of personal gain. The role of money and economic life have grown out of all proportion as an all-consuming cancer. Art has become frivolous and superficial. The mysterium has been banished and replaced by liberal 'ethics', destroying or corrupting not one, but every religion.

Victory over the forces of despair will mean a complete reorientation of man's outlook. Change will demand a world reflective of the original order, the cosmic order. It will be hierarchical, diverse, a social organism in which everyone has a valued role. The outlook that will prevail will be vertical in orientation. Above all, the world will be run on the principles of personal fulfilment and salvation, rather than the money-lending principle of greed.

The economy will exist to serve the people and capital to serve the economy. Today it is the other way around: ordinary people, especially the millions and millions of migrant workers, exist for the sake of the economy and the economy exists to serve capital.

Karl Marx perpetuated a lie when he obliterated the difference between capital and the economy. The effect of his doctrine was to pit workers against employers and distract them from the depredations of banking capitalists, who live from usury. The truth is that, behind the smoke-screen false dichotomies of worker versus employer, or worker versus worker in the degrading and dehumanising slave or jobs market, the essential economic dichotomy is usurers versus everyone else.

Marx disguised the fact that under the system of interest slavery, the employer is required to deal in money that has to be repaid with interest. Under this system the capitalist is not the employer who creates the basis for the worker's existence, but rather the money-lender.

By lending money, the Usurocracy triumphed everywhere in the world, thanks to the fact that they held the monopoly over the worlds exchange currencies, first in the form of currencies backed by gold and now in the form of the dollar.

A traditionalist world will abandon this financial tyranny, with the result that there will be no international trading credits or a reserve currency, with lost billions upon billions in private profit from interest on international indebtedness.

Labour creates value, not gold. A traditionalist economy will return to work and production rather than usury and speculation. Money needs to be backed by nothing other than productive labour. Once this is understood, the requirements of an economy are relatively simple; as simple as A B C argued Ezra Pound. Money becomes 'a certificate of work done'. The work done 'must be necessary' and 'there must be some way for everyone to get enough money... to satisfy a reasonable number of lacks. The simplest road is through work'.[78]

In addition to Pound, the unifying principle of thinkers such as Gottfried Feder, C. H. Douglas, Silvio Gessel, Margrit Kennedy and others is that they have all eschewed the usurious lending and the fractional reserve banking that established Usura in its position of world domination in the first place. Starting from the principle

---

[78] Pound, *ABC of Economics*, p,51.

that the economy exists to serve rather than be served, their common objective has been to rein in the runaway power of money, an objective that would have been shared with enthusiasm by attendees of the church councils in the high Middle Ages.

28   Simone Weil on the social organism

A social organism that is true to tradition can only be founded on the principle of unity in multiplicity, with all contributors through labour considered as equally important to its progress. Everyone must be active, through a shorter working day if necessary. The degrading and brutalising slave or jobs market would have to go. Everyone, everything, must be considered to be in a relationship with someone or something else in conformity with their respective natures, and thus in conformity with the right to fulfil those natures. This right is not expressed as an absolute, as it is under liberalism, but as a relation.

Simone Weil expressed this insight in *The Need for Roots*,[79] her blueprint for a new post-World War II social organism. She wrote that 'a right is not effectual by itself, but only in relation to the obligation, the effective exercise of a right springing not from the individual who possesses it, but from other men who consider themselves as being under a certain obligation towards him'. Her point was that it is the relative nature of a right which makes it

---

[79] First published in 1949 as *L'Enracinement* and in English translation with T.S. Eliot's preface in 1952 as *The Need for Roots*.

effective. 'An obligation which goes unrecognised by anybody', she wrote, 'loses none of the full force of its existence. A right which goes unrecognised by anybody is not worth very much'.[80] Under liberalism, it is the one-sided understanding of each right as an absolute and possessed equally by everyone, that has actually destroyed rights, i.e. the right of a nature to be what it is.

'Rights', Weil wrote, 'are always found to be related to certain conditions. Obligations alone remain independent of conditions. They belong to a realm situated above all conditions, because it is situated above this world'.[81]

'The men of 1789' (in other words Weil meant the progenitors of modern liberalism), 'did not recognise the existence of such a realm. All they recognised was the one on the human plane. That is why they started off with the idea of rights. But at the same time they wanted to postulate absolute principles. This contradiction caused them to tumble into a confusion of language and ideas which is largely responsible for present political and social confusion'.[82]

Weil was making the point that it is a belief in a 'realm situated... above this world' that will determine whether

---

[80] Simone Weil, *The Need for Roots*, Routeledge and Kegan Paul, Abingdon, 2008, p.3

[81] Weil, p.4

[82] Weil, p.4

or not men will submit willingly to the obligations of the social organism. Such a submission will demand a reorientation of all values to the vertical, rather than a horizontal human plane, where submission to a higher principle is necessary if rights are to mean anything at all.

Nevertheless, the prevailing view in the West is that there is a hierarchy of sorts in the modern democracies, a hierarchy founded on individual merit. This attempt, however, to render equality and difference compatible reflects the 'political and social confusion' that Weil observed. Meritocracy justifies differences of social status defined quantitatively by wealth, by money, in a world where money makes more money. It also encourages the perversity of individuals who strive to be materially different, whether for honour, reward or survival, which has led to a world of increasing sameness, uniformity and conformity. To apply wealth as the defining factor circumscribes status within the measure of human estimation, to that which is easily calculable. It renders beings uniform, so that there can never be anything singular. Everything, everyone, now conforms with the standard of universal measurement. 'Money destroys human roots', exclaimed Weil, 'wherever it is able to penetrate, by turning desire for gain into the sole motive. It easily manages to outweigh all other motives, because the effort it demands of the mind is so very much less. Nothing is so clear and so simple as a row of figures'.[83]

---

[83] Weil, p.44

Not surprisingly, Simone Weil expressed economic activity as being subordinate to 'the needs of the soul'. In addition to the necessity of obligation, she also cited order, obedience and hierachism as essential to the soul's well being. Equality was included in her list too, but this was not the destructive 1=1 equality of liberal ideology. Weil was specific in recommending that a 'way of rendering equality compatible with differentiation would be to take away... all quantitative character from differences'. In Weil's vision, natures would have access to a qualitative equality as souls, not horizontally amongst themselves, but vertically with regard to God.

29 T.S. Eliot and Little Gidding: a symbol of resistance

T.S. Eliot wrote a laudatory preface to the English edition of Simone Weil's *The Need for Roots,* and it is not hard to see why he was an admirer of Weil's work. He had written previously of a return to Christianity as the basis of the social organism. A society founded on the Christian ethos would 'compel changes in our organisation of industry and commerce and financial credit' and it would facilitate rather than as at present impede, a life of devotion for those capable of it.[84]

In seeking an alternative to liberalism, Eliot shared Weil's view that the economic and political must be considered as subordinate to the 'realm situated... above this world'. 'For myself', he wrote, 'a right political philosophy came more and more to imply a right theology – and right economics to depend upon right ethics...'[85]

---

[84] T. S. Eliot, *The Idea of a Christian Society,* Faber and Faber, London, 1939, p.11

[85] T. S. Eliot, 'Last Words,' *The Criterion,* January 1939, quoted in N. Khagendra Singh, *T S Eliot: a Reconsideration,* APH Publishing Corporation, New Delhi, 2001, p.60

The last vestiges of the traditional order, where money-dealing was condemned and faith was interwoven in the social fabric, had been destroyed by liberalism to be replaced by commoditisation and the cash relationship. The resultant emptiness, a form of Kierkegaardian despair, is clearly discernible in poems such as the *Wasteland* and *The Hollow Men*, and is always in tension with a hunger for meaning and a dormant metaphysical purpose. From the early work mentored by Ezra Pound, to the *Four Quartets*, Eliot illuminated the idea that life is spiritually barren and meaningless without an over-arching quest, sensibility or teleology.

In his two books of cultural criticism, T. S. Eliot explicitly acknowledged the importance of Christopher Dawson's work to his own ideas. The Preface to *The Idea of a Christian Society* (1939) singled out 'Mr. Christopher Dawson's *Beyond Politics*' as a book to which 'I owe a great deal'. In the Preface to *Notes Toward the Definition of Culture* ten years later (1949), Eliot wrote, 'Throughout this study, I recognise a particular debt to... Mr. Christopher Dawson'. Not surprisingly, given these acknowledgments, Eliot's thinking in these major works of cultural criticism was indeed very close to Dawson's.

As much as Christopher Dawson was a historian, he was even more a cultural critic searching for historical answers to the crises of modern times. He remained a relentless critic of industrialism, urbanism, and acquisitive capitalism - all the forms of materialism which he believed were at the root of modern disorders. To these he opposed the Catholic idea of a universal spiritual society *(reflecting cosmic harmony)* and, without idealising the Middle Ages, believed that this universal society had come closest to realisation during the thirteenth century, its agonised death prolonged over four hundred years since that time. Understanding this of Dawson helps in the understanding of why Eliot ended his serious poetic career with Little Gidding as his subject.

Little Gidding the poem was completed by Eliot in 1942, arguably the turning point in the Second World War. And what Eliot saw on the horizon was the victory of modernity, secular liberalism and the Americanism from which he had fled to the false sanctuary of Europe.

'You are here to kneel', said Eliot. You are here to submit to another order of things, beyond the temporal, - 'here', at 'the intersection of the timeless moment'; an order better understood by those here before you, 'where prayer has been valid'. Eliot was referring to the Little Gidding community of Nicholas Ferrar's day, a social organism founded on faith and centred on prayer. Ferrar, the former man of business, had escaped to this place from the world of commerce that was burgeoning in the Calvinistic aftermath of the Reformation. Little Gidding was the first religious house to be formed after the traumatic suppression of the monasteries during the Reformation. The devotional adherence to older forms of piety, such as round-the-clock prayer vigils, and to relics of the old religion such as crucifixes or madonnas, attracted the unwelcome attention of the Puritans, who branded Little Gidding an 'Armenian nunnery' and levelled it to the ground in 1647. This history rendered Little Gidding symbolic of the religious, cultural and political convictions held by Eliot and influenced by Dawson.

Eliot's alternative to the dissolutive impact of liberalism was the basic social unit that he identified in England as the parish, a 'unitary community' of a 'religious-social' character, which has been undermined by industrialism and urbanisation.

In *The Idea of a Christian Society*, Eliot described the parish as:

> *a small and mostly self-contained group attached to the soil and having its interests centred in a particular place, with a kind of unity which may be designed, but which also has to grow through generations. It is the idea, or ideal, of a community small enough to consist of a nexus of direct personal relationships, in which all iniquities and turpitudes will take the simple and easily appreciable form of wrong relations between one persona and another.*[86]

---

[86] T. S. Eliot, *The Idea of a Christian Society*, p.31

Eliot could have been describing Little Gidding here. It remained, for Eliot, 'now and in England', a 'thin place'[87] through 'which the purpose breaks' - the transcendent purpose of God. In the Dawson-influenced mind of Eliot, it was these religious connotations that left Little Gidding also highly charged symbolically with political and cultural significance. The poem is thus one of resistance, in which Eliot sought to plant a lasting legacy of ideas and symbols for revival by future generations. Whilst his social and political ideas were dealt a death-blow by the war, he still saw fit to smuggle something of the redemptive history and symbolism of Little Gidding into the post-war world of victorious modernity: a 'midwinter spring' in the 'dark time' of liberalism and continued decline.

---

[87] The wonderful expression coined by George McLeod, the founder of the Iona Community.

30 Ezra Pound and the triumph of the sacred force

A profound difference between Eliot and Ezra Pound was that, whilst sharing the same sense of emptiness and despair about mechanistic and materialistic modernity, Pound was not limited by the exoteric forms of religious belief. Throughout *The Cantos*, Pound grappled with the central dichotomy of our times and all times. He represented 'Usura' in the imaginative world of *The Cantos* as 'the evil, fatal force which stands in diametrical opposition to the energeia or creative, vital force derived from the contemplation of the "unity of the mystery"'.[88] Pound was always transforming the terms of the 'Usura'/ 'mysterium' antithesis, so that the single antithesis developed a polymorphous, proliferating pattern. The protean nature of this antithesis allowed Pound to express its centrality to all aspects of the human condition: mythical, cultural, historical, religious, and economic. In a *Visiting Card* (1942), Pound described historical events and conditions as products generated through the interaction of the two antithetical forces:

---

[88] D. P. Tryphonopoulos, *Ezra Pound and the Occult*, Wilfred Laurier University Press, Ontario, 1992, p.3

We find two forces in history: one that divides, shatters, and kills, and one that contemplates the unity of the mystery...

There is the force that falsifies, the force that destroys every delineated symbol, dragging man into a maze of abstract arguments, destroying not one but every religion.

But the images of the gods, or Byzantine mosaics, move the soul to contemplation and preserve the tradition of the undivided light.

The central antithesis is found in Pound's *Canto 51*, where the opposition is between the forma 'That hath the light of the DOER' and the 'sour song' arising from the belly of the usurious Geryon. The sterile, labyrinthine, blurring, destructive, dark, hylic force, which Pound identified with usury and personified as 'Usura' or 'Geryon', was in a perpetual struggle with the sacred, fecund, clear, dynamic force identified with the 'unity of the mystery,' and symbolised by the 'tradition of the undivided light'.[89]

It was the triumph of the sacred force that Pound sought. In the revolution against Usura, nothing short of this would do. He would certainly have been sympathetic to the later ideas of Roger Garaudy, who wrote:

The only possible revolutions are those which don't exclude mankind's transcendent dimension; which

---

[89] Tryphonopoulos, pp. 2-3

*don't exclude the divine; which are founded on this
article of faith; that the basic foundation of reality is
an act of the creative freedom which is called God.*

*To be a revolutionary is to be a creator of that
reality, to participate in divine life.*[90]

Once the central antithesis is understood. Once the disinformation about fighting for freedom, democracy and
human rights is cleared away. Once the war for the world
is revealed as that which it always was - a war between
the forces of good and evil - then can the sides be chosen
without ambiguity.

For only an alliance of the sacred will be able to stand up
to the empire of the profane. Only a coalition of believers
in mankind's transcendent dimension has a hope of
combatting amoral liberalism.

The perennialism and traditionalism of thinkers and
writers such as René Guénon, Julius Evola and Frithjof
Schuon provide one possible basis for such an alliance.
They held that life should be led in the knowledge of
values that originate in the transcendent reality that lies
outside of human existence, even if that absolute truth
was made manifest in different religious forms. They
pursued a shared esotericism, regardless of the exoteric

---

[90] Quoted in B. Moitessier, *Tamata and the Alliance,* Sheridan House,
New York, 1995, p.333

expression, be it Muslim, Christian, Judaic, Hindu and more.

Agreement upon the origin of values in the absolute is important, because it clearly demarcates the beliefs of traditionalist from their humanist opponents who, by cutting themselves off from the transcendent, live by human values alone. To this human-centred way of thinking, all being is understood as resource to be exploited, and this includes the ubiquitously named human resources. Without absolute values in which to ground our lives, man is subject to any form of indoctrination that a worldly power, currently the money power, might find to its advantage.

'For this I was born, and for this I have come into the world, to bear witness to the truth...' The pragmatic Pilate responds to these words of Jesus with the question 'What is truth?' Subjectivism and moral relativism were betrayed in the very question. They were prominent too in the pharisaic self-righteousness, or human-centredness, of the Jews who, together with Pilate, spurned the truth in condemning Christ.

Contrary to such dangerous relativism, the central idea of perennialism is that absolute truth is one, timeless, and universal, and that the different religions are but different languages expressing that one truth. Out of the thinkers who understand this will a gnostic leadership be drawn, which will hold good to this vision and lead us down the authentic paths.

Of course, the corrupted religious leaderships which have embraced liberalism as their core ethic will exclude themselves from any projected holy alliance. In the Christian tradition, this will mean that any support for an alliance must emerge from westerners for whom the Gospels are but a dim and distant folk memory, but who yet hold on to a belief in the transcendent nature of truth.

At least let us postpone the religious wars for the future. Right now, a bigger war must be fought, to save religion per se from destruction at the hands of the money-lenders. It will be a war for a multipolar order, respectful of hierarchy, diversity and the traditions of religious expression, an order that consciously seeks to reflect the cosmic order here, on earth. Only in such a way will resistance be offered to the empire: the unipolar giant enterprise, run by the central bank of central banks, which brutalises the dumb masses, crushing diversity under the principles of corporate HR. The prize is great, for the goal is the reclamation of our right to being, right to reality, right to authenticity.

31 Ecstasy and openness to truth

The destruction loosed upon the world by the traffickers of money led to a corrupted understanding of being, which tore men away from their oneness with the world, an integration and an experience that was immediate. Truth was once the self-disclosure to man of the things around him. The fact that man represented the revealed truth symbolically did not make the symbols arbitrary acts of the imagination, on the contrary, they remain testament to man's former openness to truth.

The mystery of the shepherding and symbolising life was shattered by a distanced imposing of 'truth' as humanity conceives it, from the minds of men, upon the world. This humanism gained credence as it developed into the Cartesian dualism of philosophy, science and art - the outlook of the modern world no less.

Humanism and liberalism go hand in hand in their belligerent and totalitarian attitude towards being, making the modern era the culmination of Nietsche's will-to-power, what Kierkegaard would have described as the apotheosis of defiant despair.

The humanist liberal eschews an integration into the world, preaching an apartness, taking the view that the free unfolding of the will, self-determination, is at the heart of what it means to be human. This observation of the world from a distance allows the self-determining individual to break things down, measure them, quantify them, work out how to exploit them and, ultimately, calculate their price. Here indeed are the principles described by Marx as Judaic, so essential to 'the pursuit of one's own advantage'.

The result is fragmentation, the force in history that *'divides, shatters, and kills'*,[91] and renders the true reality as an idea, the individual's idea, from the individual's perspective. This wilful imposition of the self, however, leaves the individual cut off from being and does not allow being to be. The smoke haze of the Cartesian opiate, in what is tantamount to a rejection of truth, fogs the objective nature of things, rendering truth relative and dependent upon each of our hallucinatory perspectives.

To the clear cast of mind that once defined original justice as order and original sin as disorder, or a rebellion against the cosmic hierarchy, then liberal humanism is blind disorder lived as order, taken to the extreme. This leaves the opposition to liberalism with the objective of a realignment to the cosmic order, which will entail an historic turn against humanism. Here lies the truly explosive

---

[91]Ezra Pound quoted in Tryphonopoulos, p.2

implication of Heidegger's life-project. Rather than being 'freed' from social obligation, to exist apart from the world in a state of subjectivist pathos, condemned to understand the world from a distance, subject and predicate would be reversed. It is in this turn, this reversal, that the way lies towards the unconcealment of the truth, or Aletheia, as Heidegger described it.

But it will first need the rebuilding of the social organism and recreation of the conditions of life in which openness to Aletheia is possible. Only then will the self-disclosure to us of the things around us once more be a real possibility. Our challenge will be to shepherd and nurture that disclosure without destroying it in the way that liberal humanism has done.

This will mean a return to the concealed truth that our technological age has covered over by treating everything as resources, including human resources. The turn against humanism will not mean the discarding of technology, after all technological innovation is itself a creative act. There will be, rather, a sensitivity to the truth, that which has been disclosed by the creation and use of the technology. Being has granted us marvellous new means by which we are able to ignore being. It is our historic task to turn those moments into unconcealment once more. Technology itself, the fulfilment of all that is wrong under liberal humanism, is the very place to look and try to understand what we have forgotten and what has been concealed from us.

Heidegger believed that we must return to the ancient Greek notion of techne, the spirit of art, technical skill and craft. He explained in *The Question of Technology* how the concept of techne preceded the historic separation of fine art and utilitarian creation, a bifurcation that was accelerated by the Renaissance. In this essay on technology, he opened a way in which the fragmentariness of human activity might be overcome, returning us to the point where life in any activity can be lived as art, lived as rite, suppressing the humanist urge to flight, enabling life to be lived before death, before the Creator.

> *But where danger is, grows*
> *The saving power also*

These lines from from Hölderlin's poem, quoted in *The Question of Technology*,[92] are central to Heidegger's hope for a salvific power in techne. It is 'the essential unfolding of technology' that 'harbours in itself what we least suspect, the possible rise of the saving power'.[93]

His hope was founded upon the truth that the humanist violence inflicted upon nature through technology can only ever be fleeting in cosmic terms. Technological innovation will only suppress the truth for so long before it metamorphoses into an instrument of catastrophic

---

[92] Heidegger, *Basic Writings*, p.333

[93] Heidegger, *Basic Writings*, p.337

revelation. It is in the very challenge to the cosmic hierarchy itself that the finitude of beings is disclosed.

The forms violently imposed upon nature as technology, in what is the vulgar conception of progress, inevitably succumb to nature's vengeance. Whilst the truth of being might be temporarily concealed in man's enslavement to technology, what is authentic, what is primal, will be reasserted and come to light. It would be at such a moment of disclosure that man will cease to challenge the hierarchy of being, taking, instead, his place within it.

> *Man is not the lord of beings. Man is the shepherd of Being. Man loses nothing in this 'less'; rather, he gains in that he attains the truth of Being. He gains the essential poverty of the shepherd, whose dignity consists in being called by Being itself into the preservation of Being's truth.*[94]

Man will regain the truth lost when floundering on the horizontal plane, by taking his place once more in the vertical order. The problem with the modern age is that a vulgar 'Ascent of Man' conception of progress dominates. The imposition of human artifice upon being is accepted as permanent and even cumulative in its growth and dominance. Heidegger challenged this popular and arrogant conception, switching the emphasis instead from the permanence seemingly exuded by technology,

---

[94] Heidegger, *Basic Writings*, p.245

toward the fleeting and violent nature of techne, best understood in the context of his words from the 1933 rectoral address: 'All that is great stands in the storm'.[95]

The fact that the storm will eventually bring everything down is lost to the everyday consciousness of the modern mind, because technological activity is radically trans-formative, challenging the nature of materials in the quest for cost reduction, performance and durability, causing artefacts to limit, rather than disclose the truth of being. This contrasts with previous ages in which the craftsman worked in cooperation with the nature of materials, which were left with their natural imperfections and temporal qualities readily apparent.

In another nod of recognition to the metaphorical powers of Hölderlin, Heidegger wrote 'Enframing blocks the shining-forth and holding sway of truth'.[96] Heidegger had in mind here Hölderlin's poem 'Autumn', the first line of which reads, 'Nature's gleaming is higher revealing'. In contrast with the ancient techne, which once disclosed, modern technology now enframes, preventing the 'higher' revelation of truth. As a result, the fleeting nature of existence is out of sight and out of mind. The 'higher revealing' is lost to human consciousness, blocked by the idea of how we wish the world to be.

---

[95] M. Heidegger, 'The Self-Assertion of the German University', trans. K. Harries, *Review of Metaphysics 38* (1985), p.480

[96] Heidegger, *Basic Writings*, p.333

Oblivious to this loss, we then set off to transform the world to make it comply with the ideas we have for it. Through the Cartesian lens, nature is conceived as raw material, ready to be moulded and shaped in any way we see fit; and this includes the human raw material, with Rousseau's 'perfectibility of man' at the heart of liberal humanist ideology in all its variants. Man himself is now an object to be shaped in the image of the liberal ideologue, 'educated' into malleability, performance-tested and constantly monitored along the road to complete 'perfection'.

In the later essay, *The End of Philosophy and the Task of Thinking*, Heidegger made the highly prophetic claim that cybernetics or information technology is the final fulfilment of the humanist concealment of truth. It is the essence of the 'will to power', an understanding of reality as pure information. Is not information, after all, something immediately accessible to the mind? Understanding being as if it were really information is, in the Cartesian sense, finally accepting true reality is an idea. Heidegger's legacy to the world is the discrediting of this humanist arrogance.

Information technology completed the western search for power over being, substituting the idea for being itself and reifying the concept as an entity. In this reduction of the world's diversity to the binary system, the final victory of quantity over quality, that began with money and the usurpation of the cosmic order by the worldly order, we have witnessed the the apotheosis of humanism, epitomised in our own time by the all-seeing and information-hungry surveillance state. Under this regime, there can be no higher good directing our making, moulding and shaping. There can only be the 'mundane principles' of liberal humanism and its earthly god - money. Everything, everyone, now conforms with the standard of universal measurement. 'Money destroys human roots', wrote Simone Weil, 'wherever it is able to penetrate, by turning desire for gain into the sole motive. It easily manages to outweigh all other motives, because the effort it demands of the mind is so very much less. Nothing is so clear and so simple as a row of figures'.[97]

We have been taken to the brink. There is nowhere left to go, but back. But how will any movement for change be able to get people to think anew, in the manner of the Shepherd? The answer has to lie in the realisation that modern, liberal, humanist rationality does not have any legitimate foundation. That which controls us is an edifice built on sand. That to which we are in thrall is ultimately money, Mammon. It all started with money.

The step back will not be easy. The money power controls education and the media. The twin pillars of Usura, the control of money supply and military might cannot be tackled head-on. The vulnerability of liberal humanism, however, lies in the shallowness of its foundations.

---

[97] See above, note 78

Once people know that 'their history' has been written by the paid servants of the money power, once education is understood as indoctrination in the interests of the money power, once science is exposed as the servant of the money power - then the edifice will eventually begin to crumble, hollowed out to the last remaining thinnest of its veneers. Once the tyrannic hold of liberalism's ideology over hearts and minds is released, the empire of Usura will come crashing down. And once the dust has begun to settle on the ruins of the prison, authentic lives will be possible once more. For this will not be progress, it will be a return to thinking as the opening of aletheia, the unconcealment of being which is the source of both being and thinking.

Such thinking is ecstatic or, to apply the translation of the Greek, is being outside the self. Salvation will be found external to man, which is what Heidegger meant in his exclamation that 'only a god will save us'.[98] The whole method of thinking that imposes concepts of the self upon being will be rejected in favour of a re-engagement with the world and immersion once more in a hyper-realism that can only be expressed in symbolic form, in ways that are no longer propositional. Instead of being expressions of subjectivist pathos, art and poetry will symbolise the moment of the revelation of being. Out of this challenge will emerge the new seriousness in art, to

---

[98] Martin Heidegger, Der *Speigel Interview,* 1966, p.11, http://web.ics.purdue.edu/~other1/Heidegger%20Der%20Spiegel. pdf , citation dated 13.12.13

replace the frivolous and purposeless expressions of self, which is lumped together as contemporary culture. In a return to techne, life itself will be lived in a state of ecstasy, as art, as rite, with no separation of the spiritual and the utilitarian. The rift introduced by the traffickers of money will be healed.

All authentic action will serve to unconceal the truth. 'And you shall know the truth, and the truth shall make you free.' (John 8:32)

Bibliography

L. Bergeron, *France Under Napoleon*, trans. Robert R. Palmer, Princeton University Press, 1981.

M. W. Bloomfield, *The Seven Deadly Sins,* State College Press, Michegan, 1952.

J. Borella, *The Secret of the Christian Way,* State University of New York Press, New York 2001.

H.V. Bowen, *War and British Society 1688-1815,* Cambridge University Press, Cambridge, 1988.

C. A. Cerami, *Jefferson's Great Gamble: The Remarkable Story of Jefferson, Napoleon and the Men behind the Louisiana Purchase,* Sourcebooks, Illinois, 2003.

King CHARLS HIS SPEECH, Made upon the SCAFFOLD At *Whitehall*-Gate, Immediately before his Execution, On Tuesday the 30 of *Ian*. 1648, VVith a Relation of the maner of his going to Execution, Published by Special Authority. London: Printed by *Peter Cole*, at the sign of the Printing-Press in Cornhil, near the Royal Exchange. 1649.
See http://anglicanhistory.org/charles/charles1.html , citation dated 5.2.14.

Count Cherep-Spiridovich, *The Secret World Government or 'The Hidden Hand'*, The Anti-Bolshevist Publishing Association, New York, 1926.

G. M. Coogan in *Money Creators*, Sound Money Press, Chicago, 1935.

Dante, *Paradiso: Third Book of the Divine Comedy*, trans. A. Mandelbaum, University of California Press, New Jersey, 1984.

E. Duffy, *The Stripping of the Altars: Traditional Religion in England c.1400 - 1580*, Yale University Press, 2005.

T. S. Eliot, 'Last Words,' *The Criterion*, January 1939, quoted in N. Khagendra Singh, *T S Eliot: a Reconsideration*, APH Publishing Corporation, New Delhi, 2001.

T. S. Eliot, *The Idea of a Christian Society*, Faber and Faber, London, 1939.

P. Elliott, *Ceremonies of the Liturgical Year: According to the Modern Roman Rite*, Ignatius Press, San Francisco, 2002.

J. Evola, *Revolt Against the Modern World*, Inner Traditions International, Vermont, 1995.

J. W. Foster, *A Century of American Diplomacy 1776-1876*, Houghton Mifflin, Boston, 1900.

J. A. Garfield, *Inaugural Address,* Friday, March 4, 1881, quoted on http://www.bartleby.com/124/pres36.html Citation dated 29.11.13.

M. Heidegger, D*er Speigel Interview,* 1966, p.11, http://web.ics.purdue.edu/~other1/Heidegger%20Der%20Spiegel.pdf , citation dated 13.12.13.

M. Heidegger, *History of the Concept of Time: Prolegomena,* Indiana University Press, 1992, p.291.

M. Heidegger, *Letter on Humanism,* in *Basic Writings,* ed. David Farrell Krell, Routledge, Kegan and Paul, Abingdon, 1978.

M. Heidegger, 'The Self-Assertion of the German University', trans. K. Harries, *Review of Metaphysics 38* (1985).

C. Hollis, *Two Nations, A Financial Study of English History,* George Routledge and Sons, 1935, London.

Johnsoniana: Anecdotes of the Late Samuel Johnson LL.D, Mrs Piozzi, Richard Cumberland, Bishop Percy and others together with the diary of Dr Campbell and Extracts from that of Madame D'Aeblay newly collected and edited by Eobina Napier, London, George Bell and Sons, York Street, Covent Garden, and New York, 1892.

S. Kierkegaard, *Provocations: Spiritual Writings of Kierkegaard*, C. E. Moore ed., Plough Publishing, New York, 2002.

D. Landes, *Dynasties: Fortune and Misfortune in the World's Great Family Businesses*, Penguin, New York, 2007.

B. Lang, *Philosophical Witnessing: The Holocaust as Presence*, Brandeis University Press, 2009.

S.P. Marron, 'Henry of Ghent and Duns Scotus on the Knowledge of Being', *Speculum*, The Medieval Academy of America, Cambridge, Massachusetts, Vol 63, No 1, Jan, 1988.

K. Marx and F. Engels, *German Ideology, Part 1 and Selections from Parts 2 and 3*, ed. Christopher John Arthur, International Publishers, New York, 2004.

K. Marx, *On the Jewish Question, Marx and Engels Collected Works*, Vol. 3, Lawrence and Wishart, London, 1975.

B. Moitessier, *Tamata and the Alliance*, Sheridan House, New York, 1995.

Critics of the Enlightenment: Readings in the French Counter-Revolutionary Tradition, Edited and translated by Christopher Olaf Blum, ISI Books, Wilmington, 2003.

M. Perry, *Sources of the Western Tradition: Volume I: From Ancient Times to the Enlightenment*, Wadsworth Cenage Learning, Boston, 2014

Ezra Pound Speaking, Radio Speeches of World War II, Edited by L. W. Doob, Greenwood Press, Westport, Connecticut and London, 1978.

E. Pound, *ABC of Economics*, Faber and Faber, London, 1933.

E. Pound, *Guide to Kulchur*, New Directions, New York, 1970.

E. Pound, *Selected Prose*, Faber and Faber, London, 1973.

F. Schoun, 'The Question of Evangelism', taken from the collection of essays entitled *Ye Shall Know the Truth: Christianity and the Perennial Philosophy*, World Wisdom Books, Bloomington, 2005.

Senate Document 23, National Economy and the Banking System of the United States: An exposition of the principles of modern monetary science in their relation to the national economy and the banking system of the United States, by R. L. Owen, United States, Government Printing Office, Washington, 1939.

R.H. Tawney, *Religion and the Rise of Capitalism*, Pelican, Harmondsworth, 1961.

A. Tinniswood, *By Permission of Heaven: The Story of the Great Fire of London,* Jonathan Cape London, 2003.
St. Thomas Aquinas, *Summa Theologica,* Question 83, Article 1, trans. Fathers of the English Dominican Province, Christian Classics Etherial Library, Calvin College, Michigan, p.931, online resource http:// www.ccel.org/ccel/aquinas/summa.pdf , citation dated 6.2.14.

J. Trachtenberg, *The Devil and the Jews,* The Jewish Publication Society, Philadelphia, 1995.

D. P. Tryphonopoulos, *Ezra Pound and the Occult,* Wilfred Laurier University Press, Ontario, 1992.

US Department of State, *Papers relating to the foreign relations of the United States, Bayard Taylor to Secretary Seward,* October 29,1862, Government Printing Office, Washington DC, 1864.

Encyclopedia of the Middle Ages, ed. A. Vauchez, R. Barrie Dobson, M. Lapidge, James Clarke and Co, Cambridge, 2000.

S. Weil, *The Need for Roots,* Routeledge and Kegan Paul, Abingdon, 2008.